THE SHOT-MAKER'S CODE

The Secrets of the Golf Stroke Revealed

Paul Byrne

The Shot-Maker's Code Ltd.

Copyright Paul Byrne 2022© All rights reserved.

No portion of this book may be reproduced - mechanically, electronically, or by any other means, including photocopying - without the express written consent of the publisher.

ISBN: 979-8-9864412-4-5

The Shot-Maker's Code Ltd.

Banchory, Scotland.

Edition No.2:

Changed Trim Size from 7"x10" to 6"x9"

Moved shot data to an Appendix

Clarified shot types in Chapter 5

For inquiries, contact

Paul Byrne <theshotmakerscode@gmail.com>

This book is dedicated to my grandson Bradley Victor Byrne

Born May 2022

Table of Contents

Acknowledgments 5

Testimonial 9

Foreword 11

Preface 13

Chapter 1: How the Journey Began 17

Chapter 2: Understanding Impact Dynamics 25

Chapter 3: The Shot-Maker's Code Blueprint 41

Chapter 4: Basic Shot-Making 59

Chapter 5: Advanced Shot-Making 73

Chapter 6: Taming the Wind 91

Chapter 7: The Modern Golf Swing 105

Chapter 8: A Short History of Shot-Making 133

Chapter 9: Mr. Hogan's Secret Revealed 145

Chapter 10: Learning Smarter 153

Summary of Key Insights 167

Final Remarks 175

About the Author 177

Glossary of Terms 179

References 193

Other Resources 195

Appendix: Chapters 4 and 5 Shot Data 197

ACKNOWLEDGMENTS

Firstly, a massive thank you to my son James, a professional golfer, former Scottish International player, Walker Cup player, and Arizona State University Sun Devil, for his immense contribution. Without his help, this book would not have been possible. He assisted in extensive range testing over several years to help with our shot data analyses and validation.

As well as critiquing the content of the book, he also filmed a full range of his golf shots, from which we were able to capture images to illustrate the book. I was delighted with the results of his work, which surpassed my expectations.

My wife, Sue, also deserves my thanks. She has patiently endured the long hours I have remained glued to my PC. Thanks to my twin brother Steve, a Chartered Engineer, for his editing skills and the excellent job he has done in challenging and testing my hypotheses on the golf stroke. We spent hundreds of hours reviewing feedback and getting the book into shape. A task made slightly more challenging as we live on different continents. Our back-and-forth discussions on every aspect of the book's content were invaluable to me. Many thanks to Michael, my nephew, for the book cover design and to my sister Hilary and her husband, James Payton, for their advice with proofreading and layout.

I have been inspired and learned a great deal from many excellent golf instructors and coaches during my journey. I want to take this opportunity to thank Murdo McCorquodale, David Naylor, John Ankenbrandt, Andrew Locke, Spencer Henderson, Neil Marr, Ian Rae, and Gregor Monks. They have each done so much to aid my son's skill development. Thank you also to Banchory Golf Club and its members for their support for James since he became a member aged eight. A big thanks to all who have helped and supported him during his amateur and professional golfing career.

Thanks to Mr. Luvin A Lim of the Wiz Golf Performance Center in Singapore, who took the time to record many hundreds of James' shots to assist with our data analyses.

I owe my thanks to the 1995 PGA Champion and Vardon Trophy Winner Steve Elkington, who kindly took the time to work with my son on the practice range and from whom I obtained many insights into shot-making. I was privileged to be present for an extended range session and gained an increased admiration for perhaps one of the most efficient and elegant golf swings.

I would also like to thank Bobby Shave and Seamus McGee, the authors of Golf Secrets Exposed and The Hershey Hurricane. They both kindly took time to share their insights into the unique talents and skills of the great American golfers Wild Bill Melhorn and Henry Picard, two of the greatest ball-strikers who inspired Ben Hogan to greatness. Adrian Leman, golf collector, historian, and Ben Hogan enthusiast, has been a constant source of encouragement. Thank you, Adrian; much appreciated.

Many other notable golf teachers and players have added to my knowledge of the golf shot. They include the late Alex Morrison, Ernest Jones, Manuel de la Torre, John Jacobs, and Leslie King, and those teaching today, Michael Hebron, Jackie Burke Jr, Martin Ayers, Edward Tischler, Mike Malaska, Pete Cowen, Luther Blacklock, Steve Gould, Butch Harmon, Kelvin Miyahira, and Bobby Clampett to name but a few. The contributions from the game's greats to improve our knowledge of the golf shot has been immense. They include the indestructible Gary Player, Jack Nicklaus, Lee Trevino, Annika Sorenstam, the late Arnold Palmer and Seve Ballesteros.

It would be remiss of me not to mention the late Homer Kelley, former Boeing engineer, for his seminal work The Golfing Machine. The TGM LLC and Mr. Kelley's acolytes, Lynn Blake, Chuck Evans, and the late Ben Doyle, deserve great credit for continuing his legacy.

The first scientific analysis made of the golf shot was undertaken by the eminent Scottish physicist Peter Guthrie Tait, at the end of the 19th Century, in honor of his youngest son Freddie, a two-time champion of the prestigious British Amateur title. The learned professor's writings have greatly helped further my understanding of spin generation and control.

Lastly, I have my friend and collaborator Todd Kos to thank for his immense contribution. Residing in State College, Pennsylvania, Todd is a keen amateur golfer and the creator of the OptimalFlight, ball flight trajectory, and OptimalStrike, ball impact analysis tools.

Todd has consulted widely on developing and designing state-of-the-art golf simulators and virtual practice facilities in many parts of the world. Todd is a computer scientist and holds a Master's Degree in Applied and Mathematical Statistics. He is an acknowledged authority on golf ball flight analytics.

I am indebted to those who kindly offered to review my book in short order, especially to Todd, for his sterling work in coordinating much of the feedback.

A special thanks to:

1. American Jeff Patterson, a former Managing Editor of Golf Digest.
2. American Bob Ockenfuss, avid Hogan researcher and co-author of 'Mind Game. Discover Your Golf Identity'.
3. American Hal Underwood. Played college golf at the University of Houston, Texas. Former PGA Tour player, runner-up in the Greater Jacksonville Open in 1971, losing a play-off to Gary Player. Winner of the 1975 Portuguese Open. Veteran teaching professional at the Deerwood Club of Kingwood, Texas. Enjoyed playing a practice round with Ben Hogan at Westchester Country Club, New York.
4. Australian Paul Smith, author of the book 4D Pyramid Coaching for Sports and Business, club fitter, mental coach, golf teacher, and entrepreneur.
5. Englishman Adrian Leman, golf historian and collector. Hogan enthusiast and researcher.
6. Englishman Michael Tweddell, veteran amateur golfer, R&A member, son of former Amateur Champion, and two-time GB&I Walker Cup Captain Dr. William Tweddell. Michael won the prestigious R&A Glennie Medal in 1962. He was presented with the medal by his father, then Captain of the R&A.

Thanks also to others I haven't mentioned who have contributed directly or indirectly. Your feedback was extremely important and insightful.

TESTIMONIAL

Approximately three years ago, the author, Paul, and I started conversing on Twitter about golf swing mechanics. I was captivated by his insights and knowledge of golf.

Paul's Great Uncle was a golf professional and club maker who served under Tom Vardon before emigrating to America in the early 1900s. His son James is a professional golfer and a former Walker Cup player; he helped his team beat a strong American team in 2011 at Royal Aberdeen Golf Club.

Paul is interested in golf science, so he has studied the swing and the golf stroke in great detail, taking them apart and rebuilding them. His book contains excellent images of James demonstrating a variety of different shots.

After about a year of exchanging messages, I thought I would try Paul's novel theories. After three months or so, I was striking and controlling my shots much more effectively, having a better understanding of the mechanics and dynamics of the swing and the stroke.

I have had many lessons from great teachers, but I found this book to be a revelation and an important breakthrough in shot-making. I would recommend it to anyone who wants to further their knowledge of the golf shot, both professionals and beginners.

I hope you enjoy Paul's passion for this great game. With his American colleague Todd Kos, I believe they found the secret that Mr. Ben Hogan dug out of the dirt after many years.

Paul and I have become great friends and continue experimenting and improving our knowledge. The Shot-Maker's Code is Paul's first book which I believe will help to transform the way golf is taught and played in the future.

Adrian G Leman.
Cobtree Manor Park Golf Club, Kent.
Golf Historian and Collector
Aged 57. Handicap 4.7

FOREWORD

"Golf is deceptively simple and endlessly complicated; it satisfies the soul and frustrates the intellect. It is at the same time rewarding and maddening – and it is without a doubt the greatest game mankind has ever invented." – Arnold Palmer

The Shot-Maker's Code is a legitimate way to make golf simpler, more soul-satisfying, and rewarding. It has impacted my game by my achieving a best-ever handicap to date. What I was doing beforehand, for thirty-four years, was a complicated exercise doomed to futility and failure.

In my ten-year journey with Paul, we have unlocked a much deeper understanding of what matters in executing the golf shot. The shot-making secrets of the golfing greats have been revealed.

You can have all the talent in the world to play the game or have all the time to practice to get very good. However, it does not mean you will ever fully understand it like the 'greats'. You could study all the best swings in the world, or analyze thousands of biomechanical data points in pursuit of the perfect swing. The one swing that matters is yours, and owning it with The Shot-Maker's Code fundamentals is all you need.

This book lays out the fundamentals so you can have a real foundation to work with and build on every time you play. I committed my game to The Shot-Maker's Code blueprint. It was transformative in creating straight and curved shots to target at different trajectories, simply and powerfully. Paul's son James has validated it with launch numbers in hand. The 'know-how' to do this is all here. My golf journey and successes can also be yours with an open mind, regardless of skill level and age.

It has been an honor and pleasure to walk this path with Paul and James to shape this code. You can put it into action and integrate it into your golf game. A great golf game awaits you.

Todd Kos
State College, Pennsylvania, U.S.A
Creator of OptimalFlight,
a Ball Flight Trajectory Analysis
and Optimization Tool

PREFACE

Several years ago, while helping my colleague, Todd Kos, develop his advanced golf impact analysis tool, we happened upon a chance discovery about the golf shot that could change how the game is taught and played. There was much more to the golf shot than we first realized, allowing us to crack The Shot-Maker's Code.

We uncovered insights into how the golf shot is performed at the highest level, information that has remained a mystery until now. We also realized that the approach isn't unique to top players; it can benefit any golfer with an open mind, prepared and willing to relearn the golf shot.

The book contains new information and insights that turn on its head the prevailing view of the golf shot. It calls into question the Ball Flight Laws, the basis for golf instruction developed by the PGA of America in 1991, which is generally the accepted global standard.

To the best of my knowledge, it is the first time that a blueprint has been created that represents the definitive design of the modern golf stroke to obtain any shot outcome. Regardless of gender or age, the reader only has to acquire the blueprint and apply it on a regular basis to experience a significant improvement in scoring and enjoyment of the game.

If you are reading this book, I would hope that you have an open mind and are prepared to apply the Shot-Maker's Code to your own game. I am confident that with only a small amount of practice, the changes you make will bear fruit.

SETTING THE SCENE

All the shots described in the book and demonstrated in the images have been thoroughly tested and validated over a period of many years with golfers at all levels. They represent the most efficient and reliable form of the golf shot and perform exactly as described. The data and flight profiles have been provided in the Appendix to the book as part of the validation.

When the shots are correctly and carefully configured and executed, they are performed as intended, regardless of the player's skill set. For those readers who don't wish to master the full range of shot types and simply want to hit longer and straighter shots more consistently, this book can help.

The Shot-Maker's Code explains how shots are curved and straightened and how the player controls the trajectory and distance of the shot.

Chapter 1 tells the story of how new insights I acquired from researching and testing the golf shot led me to write the book and document my findings.

Chapter 2 shines a spotlight on the mysteries of the dynamic relationship between the clubhead and the ball and reveals the importance of this relationship to the outcome of the shot.

Chapter 3 maps out a blueprint of the golf stroke for shot-making designed to maximize the efficiency of the energy transfer from the clubhead to the ball and enhance the player's control of the shot outcome. It shows how the stroke can be configured in advance to obtain the desired shot outcome. As part of the blueprint, by establishing stroke constants in the form of a baseline stroke, stroke variables are significantly reduced, eliminating unnecessary movement in the swing and reducing the complexity of the strike. When a baseline precision golf stroke is deployed, the swing direction and clubface angle are no longer stroke variables; they become stroke constants.

Chapters 4 and 5 demonstrate in some detail, with the help of images, how the stroke, once configured, is applied to execute a full range of different shot types.

A demonstration of the shots, with a voiceover description, can be found on the YouTube channel: The Shot-Maker's Code.

Chapter 6 explores shot-making in the wind and demonstrates how the player's control of the spin rate enables him to combat or harness the wind.

Chapter 7 describes the modern swing and stroke pioneered by the great Ben Hogan.

Chapters 8 and 9 examine the golfing greats and their approach to shot-making.

Chapter 10 contains an entirely novel approach to learning the golf shot. It concentrates on how the player learns the stroke for the shot, not the swing, as the route to developing his own shot-making skills on a path of continuous improvement.

The Appendix contains launch data and ball flight profiles for shots described in Chapters 4 and 5. The data serves to validate the Shot-Maker's Code. All the shots performed exactly as anticipated.

NOTE:

While I have tried to use reader-friendly terms, there will inevitably be many terms that you may not recognize; please refer to the Glossary of Terms for clarification. You may wish to familiarize yourself with the terms before reading the book. Also, several terms in this book may have different meanings depending on the context in which they are used. One obvious example is the term 'strike', which is used in different contexts as a noun or verb.

All references to the golf swing or grip assume right-handedness. Please reverse the reference for the left-handed player.

While playing golf and applying The Shot-Maker's Code does not depend on the sex of the golfer. I have used the male gender pronoun throughout to avoid having to use the inelegant he/she or he or she.

I hope you enjoy the book and gain real benefit from it. Thank you for taking the time to read it.

CHAPTER 1: HOW THE JOURNEY BEGAN

The author tells of the long-term collaboration with his American colleague who was developing a golf impact analysis tool. He recounts his motivation for writing the book - the breakthrough moment during the project that led to The Shot-Maker's Code.

Due to what they initially considered to be a quirk in the spin rate during range tests, they had found the key to unlocking the mysteries of the golf shot.

This quirk enabled a better understanding of the golf stroke and how it is configured. It became their focus of attention instead of emphasizing perfect swing and club geometry.

CHAPTER 1

HOW THE JOURNEY BEGAN

In 2012, two men, previously unknown to each other, embarked on a collaborative journey to analyze the golf shot. The journey would reveal insights about the golf shot, which the great ball-strikers understood instinctively but have remained hidden from most of us until now.

After witnessing my son and his golfing pals coping with powerful winds on many of Scotland's links courses, I became intrigued at how the wind affects the golf ball's flight. Having retired, I was free to investigate.

As with any technical study, I needed data and the means to analyze it. My first step in the summer of that year was to search the internet for any ball flight analysis application that could potentially help. After an extensive and exhaustive search, I found only two ball flight analysis programs capable of accounting for wind effects on the golf ball's flight. One application was best suited to the driver; the other could analyze shots produced by any lofted club (wedge to driver).

Having found what I thought would be the ideal shot analysis tool, I contacted the tool's creator and developer in the United States, Mr. Todd Kos, and explained what I was planning to do. Todd knew instantly that his ball flight analysis tool provided almost the exact fit for me and graciously agreed to help.

Our conversation moved to the science of impact. I explained to Todd that I had studied golf impact science but was keen to understand more. Specifically, I wanted to learn about the impact parameters that affected the spin rate and launch direction. I was even more curious to see how changing these might affect the ball in windy conditions.

By sheer coincidence, Todd was just about to embark on developing an impact analysis tool to complement his successful ball flight analysis program. On that very day, almost by accident, we began a part-time collaboration in support of his project development that continued almost daily for several years.

With Todd's keen scientific mind and with the help of my son James and input from interested golf teachers and others, we have tested, simulated, analyzed, and validated thousands of shot data, gaining numerous valuable insights into the golf shot in the process.

After some time into our collaboration, having puzzled over inconsistencies in impact data obtained by various launch monitors and our data, we both realized that the investigation of club and swing data could only take us so far.

After extensive research and real-world testing were done to take a closer look into golf ball spin generation, we were able to unravel the mysteries of the golf stroke. It has also enabled us to better explain Ben Hogan's secret with The Shot-Maker's Code.

With a high degree of certainty, we finally know how to configure and execute the golf stroke to obtain any shot shape or trajectory. Exciting days lie ahead in sharing these critical insights, hopefully in a way that can benefit anyone interested to learn more. Helped by science and modern technology, we have acquired the same learning that the great Ben Hogan acquired over more than ten years of hard graft, trial, and error. The process has been a similar trial of persistence, hard work, luck, and sometimes failure.

THE BREAKTHROUGH MOMENT

During the first few years of our collaboration, Todd refined club-to-ball impact formulas and developed a strike analysis tool. His objective was to formulate the impact conditions responsible for the ball's launch and spin characteristics and ball speed; to gauge how each of the parameters related to each other to obtain a comprehensive range of different shot types and ball flights.

Todd kept me in the loop on his development, and in a period of just a few years, we exchanged many thousands of messages online. The discipline of noting down our thoughts forced us to explain them in more detail and with greater clarity than we could expect from an in-person discussion.

The development of the strike analysis program was a long journey, with many encouraging moments and setbacks. The task seemed like trying to solve a Rubik's cube but thousands of times more difficult. Of course, due to the large number of variables governing the human body's motion, club-to-ball impact algorithms will not be able to account for everything, no matter how good the data.

Todd's analysis showed only a weak correlation between a divergent clubface orientation and clubhead direction to account for the spin rate and spin axis when testing the thousands of launch data. A weak association was expected for the driver and other woods, as on those clubs, an off-center hit will cause a gear effect, which will change the spin rate. However, we expected to see a good match for iron shots, so the weak correlation for irons was surprising. Either Todd's formula was wrong, or some other spin mechanism was in play. At this point, it wasn't easy to prove either case.

Previously, I had studied Professor Jorgensen's D-Plane theory of impact to understand the critical impact parameters.

The D-Plane considers vectors from the clubhead's travel direction (club path and angle of attack) and the clubface orientation (face angle and delivered loft). These vectors would be tied to launch angle and spin results. Some launch monitor manufacturers currently use this concept in their impact models from swing and club data.

My son and I spent many hours on the range, testing the validity of the theoretical D-Plane Model with intentional club path moves and swing directions. Still, our results were very disappointing, to the extent that both Todd and I were beginning to question the model's efficacy and assumptions.

One day, during range testing, the test schedule included a series of left-to-right fade shots with a 6-iron, with a stance pivoted more open. The shots produced penetrating trajectories and impressive distances. When checking the data, I noticed that the shots had much lower spin rates than other shots made with the same club.

As the clubhead speed and ball speed hadn't changed significantly, I surmised that something unexpected must have happened during impact to account for the much lower spin rate and significantly longer shots.

To find out, Todd and I had to check if there was a good correlation between the spin rate for these shots and the amount of spin loft, which is a computed, not measured, metric of the 3D divergence between the clubface orientation and clubhead direction. We found these shots were outliers; there was a significant mismatch between the spin loft and the actual spin rate.

At this point, we began our journey together to find answers. It occurred to us that we should perhaps look more closely at the ball impact geometry and dynamics rather than relying solely on club or swing geometry impact metrics.

It soon began to dawn on Todd and me that understanding the golf stroke and what was happening to the clubhead and ball during impact, rather than being overly concerned with what the swing was doing, was where our focus should be. It became a breakthrough moment. With a clearer understanding of impact dynamics and through a process of reverse engineering, the shot-making process involving the dynamics of the stroke and the strike itself would become more apparent to us. It was like removing a veil covering our eyes. We could now better account for every shot outcome.

Current golf instruction considers the swing in terms of the geometry of a circle and the physics of rotation. It prescribes the use of planes, lines, and angles designed to keep the clubhead on its ideal orbit around the body. These fundamentals are applied systematically to establish the right club and swing alignments, both at the address and during the swing itself, appropriate for the individual player and his natural swing style.

Many adherents to this philosophy have not realized that club and swing alignments measured at impact are outputs, not inputs. The swing is a natural and intuitive response to the player's intended stroke and ball flight; It reacts to what has gone before, specifically to the initial part of the takeaway and how the golf stroke had been configured during the setup.

This book describes our discovery process towards revealing The Shot-Maker's Code, which contains the secrets of the golf stroke, shot-making, and spin control.

Many of the insights will have direct and immediate relevance for the skilled ball-striker. Lesser skilled golfers will also greatly benefit from the simplified and efficient stroke fundamentals, which create further understanding of the golf shot, improved shot-making skills and increased shot distance and accuracy. In short, knowing what you are doing with The Shot-Maker's Code and possessing the full range of shots is a thousand times better and more satisfying than swinging and hoping for the best and struggling for consistency from one round to the next.

The book will answer our first question: Why should the lower spin fade shot be differentiated from many other similar shots? The reasons found within the stroke's dynamics and the ball impact geometry provided us with the blueprint for all shot-making and spin control.

My son James deserves credit for helping us test what he must have thought were our madcap ideas. We spent countless hours on the range and golf course, testing new theories and ideas about how best to control the golf ball, both the spin applied and the shot's shape and trajectory. Putting these ideas into action has been invaluable to this research, and we are grateful to him and others who have helped us in any small or large way.

CHAPTER 2: UNDERSTANDING IMPACT DYNAMICS

A deep dive into understanding the nature of impact and how the strike can be viewed as a process for fashioning shots rather than as a single instantaneous event.

The chapter differentiates the role of the forward stroke from the overall swing. It offers a fresh perspective of the golf shot that opens up opportunities for improved control of the ball flight and the shot outcome at any skill level.

CHAPTER 2

UNDERSTANDING IMPACT DYNAMICS

Based on a better understanding of how the golfer can create and change a golf ball's spin rate, this chapter marks the start of my journey to reveal how we configure the stroke and strike in advance. It considers the impact fundamentals necessary for the golf shot and contains new insights into the clubhead's dynamic relationship with the ball.

After reading this chapter, as long as you generally appreciate the golf stroke's importance in creating and controlling the ball's launch conditions, then the following chapters will, I trust, be more readily understood. Indeed, the key to the golf shot's success is how the player compresses and imparts spin on the golf ball. It marks out the true ball-striker and shot-maker from the rest of us.

"Golf is played by striking the ball with the head of the club. The objective of the player is not to swing the club in a specified manner, not to execute a series of complicated movements in a prescribed sequence, not to look pretty while he is doing it, but primarily and essentially to strike the ball with the head of the club so that the ball will perform according to his wishes." Bobby Jones, Golf is My Game, First Edition, 1959.

Harry Vardon, Bobby Jones, Ben Hogan, Jack Nicklaus, Lee Trevino, Tiger Woods, and Annika Sorenstam have all been acknowledged as exemplary ball-strikers and shot-makers. Yet, none have fully explained why and how they achieved mastery of their chosen sport.

The strange quirk in the spin rate that I wrote about in the first chapter has proven to be the key to unlocking this mystery, which I am excited to share in this book.

THE NATURE OF IMPACT

The impact duration between the clubface and the ball can be less than half a millisecond. At a clubhead speed of over one hundred miles per hour, the club and ball are in contact for less than one inch of travel of the clubhead. The entire duration of the swing is merely a fraction over one second.

The force acting on the golf ball is a large force of over one ton for a driver. The ball is deformed significantly and typically leaves a circular clubface compression mark of an inch in diameter. Because of the longer length of the club and its higher total swing weight, a long iron creates significantly more compression of the ball than a short iron.

The more downrange energy imparted to the ball, the more compressed it is by the clubhead.

Golf Ball Compression

The dynamism of the strike is the dominant influence on the ball's velocity, launch angle, and spin rate. It influences the resultant ball flight and its behavior when it lands. The material composition and elastic properties of the clubshaft, clubhead, and ball are essential components of impact dynamics.

BALL FLIGHT

Together with environmental factors, such as wind and air temperature, the ball's launch characteristics determine the shot's shape and trajectory; these are:

- Launch Angle and Direction (Vertical, Horizontal)
- Ball Spin Rate and Spin Axis
- Ball Speed

When struck, the ball continues and stays on its start line or curves away from it. There are numerous combinations of shot directions, shapes, and trajectories.

SPIN GENERATION

Due to the loft on the clubface, when the ball is struck, it spins backwards about its horizontal spin axis. The spin axis can be tilted intentionally by the impact conditions. If the spin axis is tilted to the right, the shot will also curve right. The spin imparted on the ball is a product of where on the ball it is struck and the direction and magnitude of the force imparted at that point during the entire duration of impact.

The centeredness of contact is very important; the ball must be struck with the sweet spot of the clubface. A strike off-center with the driver can significantly increase or reduce the spin rate and spin axis tilt.

The sweet spot on the clubface is where the Center of Mass of the clubhead can be efficiently projected onto the ball for maximum effect. It is normally positioned in the center of the clubface or very close to it. If the player misses the sweet spot with an off-center hit, it will change the shot direction as the clubhead is rotated or twisted by the force of the mishit. In the driver and other deep-faced clubs, because the clubhead's Center of Mass is set back some distance from the clubface, a gear effect is created, changing the spin rate and spin axis. As the ball starts to reform on the clubface, the clubhead rotates in one direction, and the ball rotates in the other, acting like two enmeshed gears.

The spin rate is also influenced by friction and the elastic properties of the ball and the clubface. Any moisture or contaminants on the clubface will reduce the spin rate. The grooves etched on the clubface of irons have only a marginal direct effect on spin generation; their main purpose is to channel water, grass, and debris away from the ball and sustain the spin rate. The clubface must be kept clean and dry to enhance spin control.

A NOVEL PERSPECTIVE OF SPIN GENERATION AND CONTROL

Golf instruction today focuses on swing and club alignments and geometry as a means of generating and controlling the spin rate and ball flight. In the PGA of America Manual of Golf 1991, the relationship between the swing path and the clubface angle is defined for shot-making.

Our analysis of thousands of shot data with every lofted club has shown that there is a weak correlation between the swing and club geometry measured at impact and the spin rate. That was to be expected for the deep-faced clubs due to the influence of gear effect; however, it was not expected with irons.

Our clear conclusion was that there must be some other means of spin generation to account for the discrepancy.

Up until very recently, scientists held the view that the golf ball acted as a rigid body. It was thought that it acquired spin when struck by sliding and then rolling before leaving the clubface.

Our research found that the prevailing view of spin generation was incomplete. We found that the ball could remain in a compressed state until it separated from the clubface, dependent upon the strike force magnitude and direction relative to the ball. The finding changed our view of the golf shot. It moved our focus away from the swing to the nature of the strike. We considered how the club could be used in various configurations to generate compression torque to control the shape and trajectory of the shot.

> The ball's launch characteristics and the resultant ball flight are influenced by the conditions of impact, i.e., the dynamic relationship between the clubhead and ball and the magnitude and direction of the compressive force. This unlocks a deeper understanding of how spin is being generated by the club.

Failure to grasp this means that whatever a golfer is trying to do with changes to swing direction, club path, or angle of attack, it will not be clear. Swinging and hoping for the best is not a real solution and is a poor foundation for building golf skills.

BALL IMPACT GEOMETRY AND DYNAMICS

While the relationship between the swing path and clubface obviously does have some influence on the spin rate, we found that the actual mechanism for spin generation is ball impact geometry and dynamics.

The ball impact geometry relates to the distance between its impact point and its Center of Mass when it deforms and reforms. Impact dynamics relates to the extent to which the impact geometry changes during impact.

If the compression of the ball is sustained during impact, the resultant spin rate is less. The ball reforms and spins as it leaves the clubface. Understanding the effect of ball impact geometry and dynamics on the resultant ball flight permits us to configure the stroke in a controlled way to shape the shot or, indeed, straighten it and control how the ball behaves when it lands. We can also take steps to avoid or mitigate potentially harmful spin effects.

Discounting the wind and other environmental influences, the resultant ball flight depends only upon where on its surface the ball is struck and how it is struck.

THE STRIKE POINT ON THE BALL AND HOW IT IS STRUCK

Due to the clubface's loft, the ball is usually struck below its equator unless accidentally 'topped'. The ball's impact point made by the clubface will vary depending on the club used. A ball struck lower down on its surface is compressed less and will generally have more spin than a higher strike point. The strike point position also defines where the ball is launched and directed in its initial flight.

A compressive force directed and extended through the ball's centerline or close to it helps maximize the ball's compression on the clubface and maximize ball speed and the shot's distance; a glancing blow will not compress the ball.

For example, when the force on the ball is directed more forwards to the target than down to the ground, the collision force is distributed higher on the ball. Because the ball has more mass closer to its equator, it can compress more and sustain the compression for longer during impact.

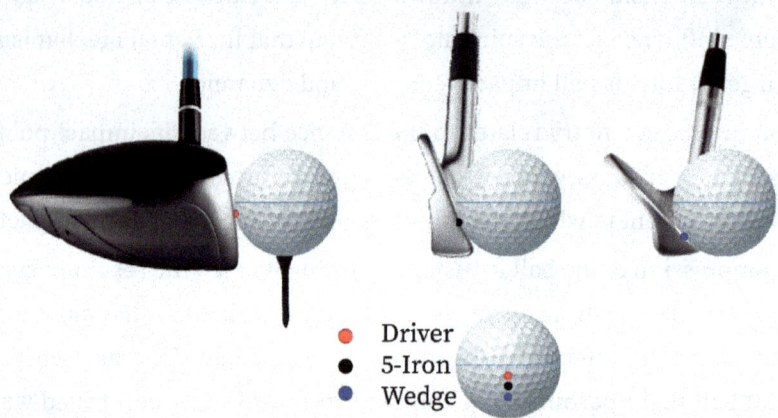

Typical Strike Points

- Driver
- 5-Iron
- Wedge

The ball's launch angle and direction are influenced by any rotation of the clubhead during its automatic release programmed during the setup. For example, if the clubhead release adds loft to the clubface, the ball will be launched higher. If it removes loft from the clubface, it will be launched lower.

Similarly, if the clubhead release rotates the clubface open or closed during impact, the ball's launch direction will change. If there is a divergence between the clubface angle and the direction of the clubhead release, the ball's spin axis will be tilted to curve the shot.

What matters is how the force is being imparted on the ball with the club, i.e., its magnitude and direction. The impact metrics attack angle and club path from launch monitors are outputs of the strike, not inputs; they may or may not align with the direction of force imparted on the ball by the clubhead.

The strike delivery on the ball is not consciously directed by the hands and arms. It is a reflexive and automatic response to a correctly configured and executed golf stroke.

THE IMPACT INTERFACE

The clubface and the ball merge during the collision as the clubhead continues on its arc of travel. The total area of the surface of the ball and clubface affected is known as the impact interface or the contact zone.

With advances in ball construction, a stable, stationary impact interface is fundamental to precision ball-striking and shot-making. The stability and robustness of the impact interface depend mainly upon the precision and solidness of the strike. It is required for every shot regardless of the desired shape or trajectory.

THE CHICKEN OR THE EGG DILEMMA

The chicken or the egg causality dilemma is stated as a question: *"Which came first, the chicken or the egg?"*

When you consider that all chickens hatch from eggs laid by chickens, the dilemma arises. Chicken-and-egg is a metaphor describing situations where it is unclear which event is considered the cause or the effect.

We can ask the same question about the golf swing and the golf stroke. Does the swing direct the stroke or vice versa? How you answer the question will depend upon your understanding of impact. Suppose you believe that the collision between the clubhead and ball is instantaneous because the impact duration is half a millisecond or less. You will also likely believe that the player can do nothing to influence it.

In that case, you will believe that conforming to a model swing is important, and configuring the swing by aligning the swing path and clubface is the key to the golf shot.

An alternate understanding of impact considers the strike a dynamic process that gives you the freedom to manufacture shots. You will believe that the stroke variability and varying the clubhead's acceleration compresses the ball to a greater or lesser degree, changing the shot's flight and outcome.

In that case, you will believe that configuring the stroke is the key to the golf shot. You will believe that the swing responds automatically, naturally, and intuitively to your intended stroke and strike.

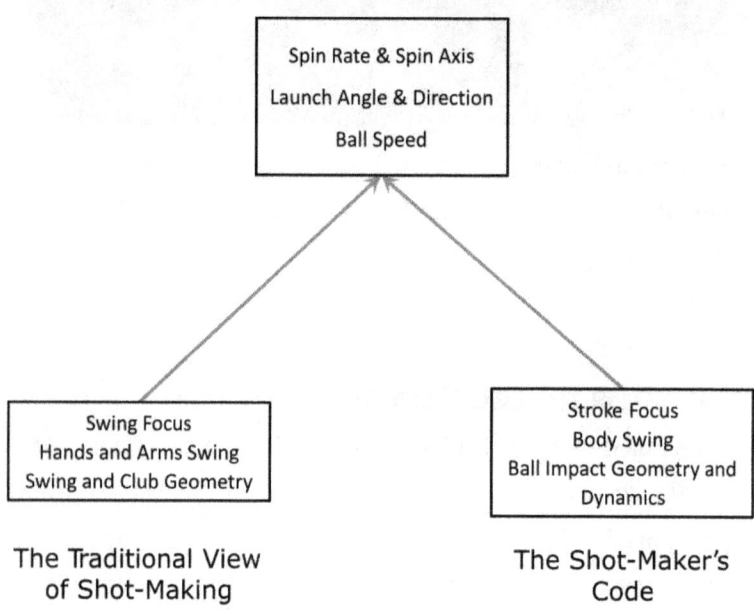

If the player swings the club with his hands and arms, he utilizes swing and club geometry for shot-making. The rotation of the arms and body must be synchronized and timed correctly to deliver the clubface correctly to the ball for the intended shot.

If the player swings the arms and club together with the powerful muscles of the body, he utilizes club and ball impact geometry and dynamics for shot-making. He configures the stroke during the setup and accelerates the clubhead's motion to compress the ball to its maximum extent. The stroke is directed forward by the right arm, not timed.

UNDERSTANDING THE MODERN GOLF STROKE

Golfers generally perceive the golf swing based on what they see and believe. A widely held view is that the club is always swung with the arms in a rotary circular motion. The modern golf stroke is not part of a circular swing; the swing's shape more closely resembles an ellipse with a wider, shallower arc, flatter at the top and bottom.

The timing of the stroke delivery on the downswing, and its extension into the follow-through, is entirely a function of the length of the takeaway before starting the upswing. In the modern swing, extending the takeaway extends the stroke beyond impact into the follow-through.

The golf stroke is analogous to the release of the clubhead, which in the modern swing begins on the downswing when the right elbow starts to uncoil. It ends when the right arm and club are fully extended at the end of the follow-through, as shown in the following graphics. The modern stroke defines the golf shot, not the swing. The swing is an automatic reflexive response to a properly configured stroke.

The red arrows on the ground line up with a tee-peg positioned a few feet ahead of the ball to mark the direction of the intended target.

At the delivery point on the downswing, where the uncoiling or unhinging of the right elbow automatically initiates the clubhead release, the player's straight left arm is naturally aligned parallel to the target line.

Subsequently, the angled straight left arm and club rotate as a single unit about the left shoulder joint to release the clubhead through impact and deliver a solid, centered strike on the ball.

Changing the downward and forward clubhead release direction relative to the slope of the ground dynamically changes the delivered clubface loft during impact to determine the ball's launch angle, spin rate, and trajectory.

The Modern Golf Stroke

Medium Trajectory Straight Shot

High Fade *Low Draw*

With a biomechanically sound left-hand grip, when the stroke is aligned to the target line at the low point of the swing arc, the clubface is delivered square to the target line for every shot.

When an on-target stroke is used, the relative position of the clubshaft tilt (forward, neutral, or rear) and strength of the right-hand grip (weak, neutral, or strong) will determine the orientation of the clubface at the initial point of impact and the ball's start line relative to the target.

With a differential right-hand grip strength and a constant left-hand grip position, the club can be used as a multi-functional tool to control the shape and trajectory of the shot.

The player must banish any idea of directing or manipulating the swing path or clubface with the hands, wrists, and arms from his mind. He must also get used to learning how to configure the stroke and not change the swing's motion, which is entirely reactive to what has gone before.

The stroke delivery is fully automated, requiring no conscious manual intervention. As The Shot-Maker's Code is revealed in this book, this last point must be indelibly imprinted in the reader's mind.

SUSTAINING THE LINE OF COMPRESSION

In 1968, Alastair Cochran and John Stobbs published their acclaimed book, The Search for the Perfect Swing. Since that time, many golf teachers have worked on various elements of their students' swings to help improve them.

Many teachers and their students are probably unaware that the secret to good golf lies not in the swing but in the stroke. The Golfing Machine, by Homer Kelley, published in 1969, stressed the importance of the line of compression, describing it as *"The Principle of Golf."* Mr. Kelley considered that sustaining the line of compression was the *"Secret of Golf."*

For a golf shot to succeed, the player must create clubhead lag and sustain stress in the clubshaft until after impact. A stressed clubshaft will sustain a horizontal straight line of compression during impact to concentrate and focus the impact forces. If the clubshaft is not stressed, the impact forces are cushioned, degraded, and scattered, leading to weak and inaccurate shots.

Clubshaft stress is created when the clubhead lags behind the grip end of the club on the downswing. In the shorter modern swing, the amount of lag tension sustained in the clubshaft is proportional to the acute angle between a line extended through the straight left arm and the club angled at the wrist. The greater this angle is, the longer the tension is sustained in the clubshaft.

The angle is established and maintained when the player deploys an extended takeaway, moving the clubhead back a short distance in a straight line ahead of the hands. The motion is an extension of the putter stroke, moving the arms and club back together as a unit.

The motion is automatically reversed at the start of the forward swing helping to compress the ball to its maximum extent and sustain the line of compression. Sighting the back of the ball, rather than the ground immediately behind it, will extend the takeaway even further and help to maximize the efficiency of the strike.

CONCLUSION

The prevailing view of impact and spin generation is incomplete. It takes little account of how the player can use stroke and strike dynamics to compress the ball and control its launch characteristics and spin rate without changing the swing speed and the resultant clubhead or ball speed. Our analyses have shown that the golf stroke's skilled design and application allow the player to determine the desired shot outcome with high precision and accuracy while maximizing the shot distance.

When we apply the Newtonian Laws of Motion to the golf stroke and strike, rather than Euclidian Geometry to the golf swing and impact, the true nature of the dynamism of the stroke and strike is revealed.

Emphasizing what has already been stated, where on the golf ball's surface it is struck and how the player compresses the ball to control the spin rate and shot trajectory is the key to the golf shot's success. It distinguishes the true ball-striker and shot-maker from the rest of us. By understanding this more in-depth, the rest of us now have an opportunity to become true ball-strikers and skilled shot-makers by applying the blueprint of the stroke for shot-making, mapped out and described in the next few chapters.

CHAPTER 3: THE SHOT-MAKER'S CODE BLUEPRINT

The chapter explains how the stroke is configured as part of the setup and takeaway process to automate the swing and strike.

The stroke parameters (constant and adjustable parameters) are established in a blueprint for the golf stroke. The chapter looks at how the adjustable stroke parameters can be combined in various ways for precision shot-making, spin and distance control.

CHAPTER 3

THE SHOT-MAKER'S CODE BLUEPRINT

Armed with our new understanding of stroke and strike dynamics, we will map out a blueprint of the golf stroke for shot-making in this chapter containing the requirements for configuring any golf shot to control its shape, direction, and distance.

The Shot-Maker's Code blueprint has two complementary features:

1. The Baseline Precision Golf Stroke - the stroke constants and prerequisites that form the foundation for every shot.
2. The Stroke Variable Adjustments - the dynamic variable stroke parameters adjusted for shot-making, spin and distance control.

The blueprint reduces the number and complexity of the interdependent stroke variables normally associated with the traditional golf swing and setup alignments. It offers a highly intelligent golf shot system that responds remarkably well to sensory feedback. In other words, it will deliver what is intended, to create a powerful dynamic golf stroke with precision and greater control of the shot's outcome.

The blueprint mapped out in the chart is not a process, method, or technique. It represents the definitive design of the golf stroke for shot-making. It is the key to the lock that will open up a whole new world of shot-making for the golfer, regardless of age or skill level. Once digested and learned, it will become second nature; the player will intuitively know how to set up for any type of shot.

The Golf Stroke for Shot-Making

```
                    ┌─────────────────────────────┐
┌──────┐            │ Environmental Factors:      │
│ Shot │ ◄──────────│ Wind, Temperature,          │
│Result│            │ Humidity, Elevation,        │
└──────┘            │ Altitude, Slope etc.        │
   ▲                └─────────────────────────────┘
   │
┌──────────────┐
│ A Dynamic    │
│ Precision    │
│ On-Target    │
│Stroke and    │
│ Strike       │
└──────────────┘
       ▲
```

┌───┐
│   Shot-Making Stroke Variable   │
│   Adjustments   │
│   ┌─────────────────────────────────────┐   │
│   │   Clubshaft Tilt Angle   │   │
│   │ (Neutral, Forward, Rear)   │   │
│   └─────────────────────────────────────┘   │
│   ┌─────────────────────────────────────┐   │
│   │   Right-Hand Grip Strength   │   │
│   │   (Neutral, Weak, Strong)   │   │
│   └─────────────────────────────────────┘   │
│   ┌─────────────────────────────────────┐   │
│   │ Sightline & Focal Point Relative   │   │
│   │   to the Ball   │   │
│   │   (Normal, Back, Top)   │   │
│   └─────────────────────────────────────┘   │
│   │
│   The Baseline Precision Golf Stroke   │
│   Constants and Prerequisites   │
│   ┌──────────────┬──────────────────────┐   │
│   │ The Clubface │   │   │
│   │ Aimed at an │   A Biomechanically │   │
│   │ Intermediate │   Sound Left-Hand   │   │
│   │ Target for   │   Grip Position   │   │
│   │ all Full   │   │   │
│   │ Shots   │   │   │
│   ├──────────────┼──────────────────────┤   │
│   │   │   An Extended   │   │
│   │ A Stable,   │   Takeaway and an   │   │
│   │ Evenly   │   Extended Clubhead │   │
│   │ Balanced   │   Release   │   │
│   │ Stance and   │   │   │
│   │ Swing   │   │   │
│   └──────────────┴──────────────────────┘   │
└───┘

THE BLUEPRINT FOR SHOT-MAKING

STANCE ALIGNMENT, BALL POSITION, AND SWING SPEED

The stance alignment and posture are not prescribed in The Blueprint for Shot-Making. The stance adjusts naturally to provide an evenly balanced and stable base for the swing.

> The ball's position in the stance is a function of how the player holds and positions the club and presents the clubface to the ball.

The swing speed is also not listed as an adjustable stroke variable. It is not strictly a setup parameter and does not need to be consciously adjusted for individual shot types. The swing speed is changed to suit the prevailing playing conditions. Otherwise, the player will optimize the swing speed intuitively to maintain the swing in dynamic balance and obtain the desired trajectory and shot distance. If an excessive swing speed disturbs the swing's dynamic balance, the result will be an inevitable two-way miss. The term 'two-way miss' means the player is missing to both the left and the right. In other words, he doesn't know which way the ball will go from one shot to the next and doesn't have control of the shot.

The two main elements of The Blueprint for Shot-Making are now explained in more detail, starting with the baseline precision golf stroke incorporating the unchanged stroke constants and prerequisites for all shots.

THE BASELINE PRECISION GOLF STROKE

When the shot is stroke-driven rather than swing-driven, a baseline precision golf stroke, overlaid on the target line, is required to guide the takeaway, the strike delivery, and the follow-through on every shot, regardless of its intended shape or trajectory.

The purpose of the baseline stroke overlaid on the target line is to ensure that the club and clubhead are correctly balanced and aligned with each other and the target at the low point of the swing arc. The club is correctly balanced when the leading edge of the clubface aligns with the centreline of the clubshaft.

A dynamically stable swing and an on-target clubhead release are automatic responses to a correctly calibrated and executed baseline precision golf stroke.

There are four stroke constants and prerequisites that form the baseline precision golf stroke and foundation for every shot.

1. The Clubface Aimed at an Intermediate Target for all Full Shots
2. A Biomechanically Sound Left-Hand Grip Position
3. A Stable and Evenly Balanced Stance and Swing
4. An Extended Takeaway and an Extended Clubhead Release

1. *The Clubface Aimed at an Intermediate Target for all Full Shots*

For all full shots, when presenting the clubface to the ball, its leading edge is aimed carefully toward an intermediate target and is kept aligned with it for the remainder of the setup. An intermediate target is a patch on the ground or a clump of grass two or three feet ahead of the ball on the target line.

On shots around the green or from greenside bunkers, the clubface may be open to the target line at address to limit the shot's distance.

2. *A Biomechanically Sound Left-Hand Grip Position*

When positioning the left hand on the club, its position must be biomechanically sound to conform to the structure of the body. For example, as the player leans forwards from the hips, the arms hang naturally and turn inwards slightly. Hence the left wrist is rotated inwards slightly when the grip is taken. The player's posture facilitates the positioning of the grip.

The left hand is positioned with the thumb down the right side of the clubshaft. When looking down, the V formed between the thumb and forefinger points approximately towards the right shoulder. The club's handle is held under the meaty pad of the palm of the left hand, running diagonally across the palm into the crook of the forefinger.

Once positioned on the club, the left-hand grip requires no further adjustment. As the left thumb sits in the cup of the right palm, it will naturally change its position on the clubshaft when the right-hand grip strength is adjusted by the player. For example, when the right-hand grip is weakened, the right palm moves the left thumb onto the top of the clubshaft. The right-hand grip strength adjustment is explained fully in the next section.

3. *A Stable and Evenly Balanced Stance and Swing*

A stable and evenly balanced stance and swing is the hallmark of the precision golf stroke.

The player must have a solid, stable base for the swing and an even weight distribution between the feet.

A change made during the setup to the player's posture, club, or grip position may require an adjustment to the stance to counterbalance the change.

Balance is maintained by pivoting the hips and stance open or closed. For example, when pivoting the stance open, the right foot naturally moves forward as the left foot is drawn back.

Fixing the chin in position at the start of the upswing and downswing limits the length of the arc of the swing, helping to keep it stable. An even tempo during the transition from the upswing to the downswing keeps the upper body stable.

4. *An Extended Takeaway and an Extended Clubhead Release*

Immediately before starting the takeaway, the player checks that the clubface is still aimed at the intermediate target.

The takeaway is initiated and extended by rotating the thoracic spine and upper torso while constraining the motion of the pelvis, hips, and lower body. Consequently, at the start of the downswing, the motion sequence is automatically reversed, with the movement and rotation of the pelvis leading the upper body rotation.

The arms and club are moved back together from the ball in a movement similar to a putting stroke. With a slight downward pressure applied on the club with the heel of the left hand to flex the wrist and straighten the arm, the clubhead moves back ahead of the hands as the player feels the heft of the arms and club. Consequently, when the clubhead is released on the downswing, the hands lead the clubhead to extend the clubhead release beyond impact into the follow-through.

The extended takeaway ends when the player's right upper arm is upright and his weight has moved over the right hip joint, at which point the player is ready to begin the uplift by coiling the right elbow and shoulder joints. The clubface is naturally slightly open to the target at the end of the takeaway without conscious manipulation or rolling of the wrists or forearms. To activate the right elbow and shoulder joints in readiness for the uplift, it is important that the right wrist and forearm are relatively 'quiet' with no sign of tension.

The club and the clubhead release is extended beyond impact into the follow-through by uncoiling the right shoulder and elbow and extending the right arm and club on the downswing. It occurs as a natural and automatic consequence of an extended takeaway. The essential movement of the extended takeaway and clubhead release and follow-through is the flattening out of the arc of travel of the clubhead.

To acquire a feel for the baseline stroke and align it with the target, the player rehearses the motion of the clubhead in the strike zone, releasing forwards towards the ball on a shallow arc along the target line.

> When an extended clubhead takeaway and release are employed, the swing direction and clubface angle, relative to the target, are no longer stroke variables; they become stroke constants for every shot.

THE STROKE VARIABLE ADJUSTMENTS FOR SHOT-MAKING

As shown in The Blueprint for Shot-Making, there are three stroke variable adjustments for shot-making and distance control, as explained below.

1. The Clubshaft Tilt Angle (Neutral, Forward, or Rearward)
2. The Right-Hand Grip Strength (Neutral, Weak, or Strong)
3. The Sightline and Focal Point Relative to the Ball (Normal, Back, Top)

When the shot is stroke-driven, the ground reaction force and the clubshaft orientation help to determine the magnitude and direction of the force imparted by the clubhead to the ball.

Tilting the clubshaft forwards or to the rear during the setup changes its horizontal orientation relative to the target and its vertical orientation relative to the slope of the ground.

As the clubface is aligned square to the target at the low point of the swing arc, as part of the baseline precision golf stroke, the variable clubshaft orientation relative to the clubface and target at impact controls the shot's direction and shape.

The launch angle of the shot is produced by the dynamic loft of the clubface at impact. The key influences on the dynamic loft are the variable forward or rearward tilt of the clubshaft, the strength of the right-hand grip, and the vertical release direction of the clubhead into the follow-through relative to the slope of the ground.

The latter defines the type of stroke, e.g., a normal stroke, a push stroke, or a cut stroke, and is facilitated by the positioning of the sightline and focal point relative to the ball.

The dynamic loft and the downward and forward direction and magnitude of the strike determine the spin rate, the shot distance, and how far the ball will roll when it lands.

In short, the relationship between the clubface and clubshaft orientation changes for shot-making. Lee Trevino was remarkably perceptive in an article in Golf Digest in 2009. He advised: *"There's no sense trying to squeeze something out of your swing if you can let your clubs do the shot-making for you."* Lee's comments mirrored those of Ben Hogan made earlier in 1948 in his book, Power Golf. *"LET THE CLUBS DO THE JOB. Instead of trying to maneuver the ball with your body, arms, and hands, trust your swing and the club you select to do the job."*

1. *The Clubshaft Tilt Angle (Neutral, Forward, or Rearward)*

When the club sits upright on its sole, the clubshaft tilt is neutral even though it naturally has a very slight forward tilt, more noticeable in the short clubs.

With the clubface aimed at the intermediate target, a clubshaft tilted forwards will reduce the shot trajectory and promote a draw; if tilted to the rear, it will increase the shot trajectory and promote a fade.

The Clubshaft Tilt Adjustment

Forward　　　　　　Neutral　　　　　　Rear

2. *The Right-Hand Grip Strength (Neutral, Weak, or Strong)*

The shot's trajectory and shape are controlled by adjusting the right-hand grip strength relative to the left-hand grip. The grip strength is the position of the grip on the club, not the degree of pressure applied by the grip to the club.

As the club is held in the root of the middle two fingers of the right hand, there is considerable scope to rotate the right wrist and grip in either direction before it is finally positioned on the club, from weak (anti-clockwise) to strong (clockwise).

The V formed by the forefinger and thumb points towards the player's left ear when a neutral right-hand grip is viewed from face-on, and the leading edge of the clubface is aligned square to the target line. To weaken the right-hand grip, the hand approaches from above the club's handle to position the grip, so the fingernails face downwards - the V points over the left shoulder. The hand approaches from below the club's handle to strengthen the right-hand grip, so the fingernails face uppermost - the V points over the right shoulder.

The Right-Hand Grip Strength Adjustment

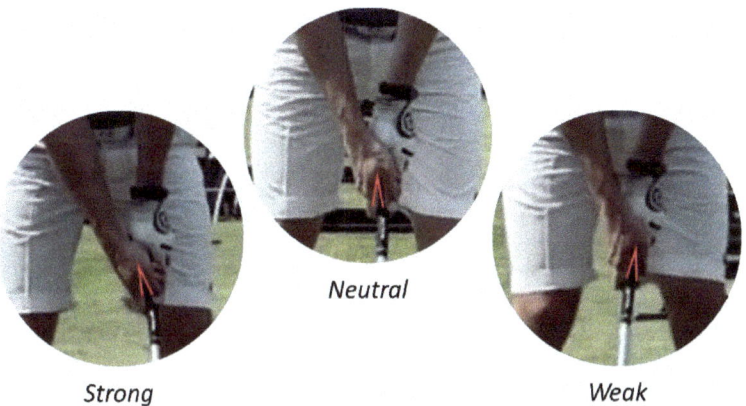

Strong *Neutral* *Weak*

The golfer must ensure both hands are matched on the club, with the Vs pointing in the same direction, to produce a straight shot of any trajectory.

When the right and left-hand grips are not matched, the shot will start its direction away from the target, relying on the baseline stroke overlaid on the target line to return it towards the target.

Knowing this allows the player to adjust to the clubshaft tilt angle and the right-hand grip strength to produce a straight shot or shape the shot in either direction and control its trajectory.

If the right-hand grip is not placed correctly relative to the left hand and the angle of tilt of the clubshaft, the result will invariably be a wayward shot.

Once the player has framed the adjustments for each shot type correctly in his mind, it then comes down to touch and feel to respond naturally and intuitively to the desired shot outcome. Hence the precise degree of adjustment of the grip and clubshaft is not prescribed.

The Shot-Maker's Matrix (Right-Handed Player)

Clubshaft Tilt Adjustment (Clubface Aligned to Target) / Right-Hand Grip Strength Adjustment		Weak	Neutral	Strong
	Forward	Low Trajectory Straight Shot	Low Trajectory Draw Shot	Medium Trajectory Draw Shot
	Neutral	Low Trajectory Fade Shot	Medium Trajectory Straight Shot	High Trajectory Draw Shot
	Rearward	Medium Trajectory Fade Shot	High Trajectory Fade Shot	High Trajectory Straight Shot

Note: The baseline precision golf stroke is the foundation for the variable stroke adjustments for shot-making.

☐ Straight Shot
▨ Fade Shot
▨ Draw Shot

3. *The Sightline and Focal Point Relative to the Ball (Normal, Back, Top)*

The sightline and focal point has three settings. The normal setting used for basic shot-making directs the sightline to a point below the back of the ball level with the leading edge of the clubface. The other two settings are used in more advanced specialty shots.

The setting is adjusted to the back or top of the ball to promote a shallower swing arc or a steeper swing arc.

A shallow arc, applied for the power stroke, allows the ball to be compressed more, minimizing the spin rate and allowing the ball to hold its line for longer. A steeper arc, applied for the laid-back cut stroke, maximizes the spin rate.

Sightline and Focal Point Adjustment

The process for configuring the constant and variable elements of the golf stroke that make up The Blueprint for Shot-Making is incorporated into the setup and takeaway process.

THE SETUP AND TAKEAWAY PROCESS

The setup and takeaway process is seamless. Its purpose is to configure and rehearse the stroke to automate the swing and strike.

The setup refers to the process the player follows to hold and position the club and present the clubface to the ball and target. A clear stroke delivery intent puts the player in the correct position to strike the ball as intended. It enables him to move seamlessly into the takeaway without any distracting thoughts.

The pre-shot routine needs only a few seconds to complete; starting the walk toward the ball to the point of impact needs only about ten seconds or slightly longer. The less complicated it is, the better the subconscious mind can order itself.

The following process describes and demonstrates the setup and takeaway sequence flow for a tee shot with a driver, done naturally and instinctively by the player. The process must have a free-flowing tempo and rhythm from start to finish; there must be no unnecessary reflection, pausing, or time-wasting.

1. The player positions the ball on the tee and sets the tee height as appropriate for the intended shot.
2. The player stands a few yards behind the ball, looking down the fairway to visualize the desired ball flight and identify where he wants the ball to land and finish. He glances back towards the ball and establishes an intermediate target positioned on the ground two or three feet ahead of it, in line with the target.
3. The player approaches the ball from the near side. His anatomy will dictate how he holds the club as he approaches the ball, i.e., with either hand or both hands. It will also dictate how he steps into his stance, i.e., first with the left foot or the right foot.
4. Sighting the intermediate target on the ground ahead of the ball, he aims the clubface's leading edge towards it as he presents it to the ball. Tilting his body forwards from the hips, he establishes the clubshaft tilt required for the shot and adjusts his grip. Any residual stress in the back, shoulders, arms, and hands is allowed to drain away. Finally, the feet are positioned, and the stance adjusts naturally to the setup to keep the body stable and evenly balanced and facilitate the release of the clubhead on a shallow arc along the target line in the strike zone.
5. Flexing the left wrist, the player lifts the clubhead a few inches off the ground to feel the arms and club's heft. Momentarily moving the right thumb and forefinger from the club's handle when lifting the arms and club helps keep the wrists and forearms free of undue tension allowing the right elbow and shoulder joints to be activated.
6. Next, he performs a 'waggle' to-and-fro to obtain a feel for the club and the intended shot.
7. Subsequently, the player tilts his head to the side and takes one final look at the target or the intermediate target before moving his gaze back to the ball. His final check is to ensure that the

clubface is set square to the target line and is aimed at the intermediate target.

When the player can 'see and feel' the shot in his mind's eye, adjusting his sightline and focal point as required, he begins the takeaway by rotating the thoracic spine and smoothly moving the club and arms back together, with the back, shoulder, and deltoid muscles. Applying slight downward pressure on the club with the heel of the left-hand lifts the clubhead from its resting position on the ground.

Hovering the driver clubhead above the ground an inch or so behind the ball will help start the clubhead back smoothly ahead of the hands and extend the takeaway, helping accelerate the clubhead on the forward swing.

If the player doesn't feel comfortable in his setup or misses a step, provided the pace of play permits, he begins the entire process again.

The sensory 'connection' between the hands, clubface, ball, and target remains throughout the swing into the follow-through.

While a full practice swing before every shot may be desirable to keep the muscles and joints free of tension and in working order, the player must rehearse the stroke and the strike to obtain a feel for it.

It is worth stressing that the player's focus is not on the swing's motion but on the direction of the clubhead's release along the target line in the strike zone.

The player's careful positioning and alignment of the clubface square to the target line and aimed at the intermediate target before starting the takeaway is crucially important. Moving the clubhead back too far outside or inside the target line will require the forward swing's compensation to correct the error. The shot outcome will be unpredictable as a result.

The Setup and Takeaway

Inattention and a lack of focus are usually the cause of a faulty takeaway. The player should not allow distractions to destroy his focus on the task.

The setup and takeaway process is critical for any club, especially the driver. When things go wrong from the tee, there is generally a fault in the setup process or an incorrect takeaway.

SUMMARY

The key elements of the modern golf stroke responsible for the control of the golf shot are:

- An on-target baseline precision golf stroke is established for every shot, regardless of its intended shape or trajectory. The player focuses on releasing the clubhead, on a shallow arc, along the target line in the strike zone, guided by the right elbow and forearm extension.
- The setup configures the stroke, specifically by how the player holds and positions the club relative to the ball and the intended target to obtain the desired shot outcome.

- The player's stance and ball position and the subsequent motion of the swing all adapt naturally and intuitively to his setup, takeaway, and strike delivery intent.
- The golf stroke is consciously formed to be subconsciously delivered.
  The shot-maker does not direct the swing or manipulate the clubface with the hands or arms.
- The swing is a reflexive, natural, and automatic response to his previously configured stroke and takeaway and the player's visualization of the intended ball flight and shot result.

CONCLUSION

Armed with the blueprint for shot-making, the player can configure the stroke to create any shot shape or trajectory and control the shot's distance and how the ball behaves when it lands with high precision. The opportunities for shot-making are limitless, bounded only by the player's skill, his 'feel', imagination, and creativity.

The baseline precision golf stroke, hereinafter referred to as the baseline stroke, is used as the foundation for every shot.

The variable stroke adjustments needed to configure the stroke for basic and advanced shot-making, and their application to several different shot types, are explained in detail in the next two chapters.

Chapter 4: Basic Shot-Making explains how the player configures and applies the stroke to control the shot's shape and direction.

Chapter 5: Advanced Shot-Making explains how the player configures and applies the stroke to control the shot's distance for long and short shots.

CHAPTER 4: BASIC SHOT-MAKING

A visual explanation and demonstration of how the blueprint for shot-making can be applied to fashion the desired shape or trajectory of the shot.

To aid a better understanding of basic shot-making outcomes, the shot data for each of the shots described in this chapter, together with ball flight profiles, are included in the Appendix at the end of the book. The data provides a powerful validation of the Shot-Maker's Code.

CHAPTER 4

BASIC SHOT-MAKING

Shaped and straight shots of varying trajectories are the subject of this chapter. To support the shot descriptions, I have included launch data, the ball flight profile, and the downrange results corresponding to each shot type described in this chapter in the Appendix at the end of the book.

The Appendix also contains a summary of data comparing all nine shots that formed the Shot-Maker's Matrix in the last chapter. The shot images and descriptions, combined with the shot launch data, provide the reader with a powerful validation of The Shot-Maker's Code.

The baseline stroke introduced in the last chapter is the foundation for shot-making; it doesn't change regardless of the shot type. As the shot-maker relies upon 'feel' and other sensory feedback, the degree of adjustment of each stroke variable for shot-making is not prescribed; each is adjusted as necessary to obtain the desired ball flight.

The setup, also described in the last chapter, does not follow a rigid method or technique on every shot. Once the club and the shot have been decided, the setup process is largely intuitive, requiring very little conscious thought to form or execute.

> To guide the setup and takeaway, the player must see the shot and its outcome in his mind's eye and have acquired a 'feel' for it. It also helps to have a mental image of the clubhead moving straight back away from the ball on the takeaway, and straight towards it and straight through it into the follow-through.

CLUB AND SHOT SELECTION FOR SHOT-MAKING

Before deciding on the club and shot to play, the player must consider the environmental factors that may influence the shot outcome, including the wind, air temperature, altitude, and elevation.

The air temperature has a significant effect on the shot's distance. More club is needed for the shot when it's cold. The player can expect to lose 15 yards on a drive and 10 yards with a short iron in near-freezing temperatures. Altitude and elevation are also factors to consider. At very high altitudes where the air is thinner, the shot will travel up to ten percent farther than at sea level.

The elevation and slope of the fairway and green are important factors, particularly on Par 3 holes and on approach shots. When the green is at a lower elevation, the shot has more time in the air and will travel farther. A shot played to an elevated green will have less time in the air.

Generally, on full shots, the player should take one club less when hitting downhill into a green and one club more when the green is elevated. In situations where the elevation is more than ten yards, the player should allow a total yardage adjustment of 0.8 yards for every one yard of elevation change.

Probably the biggest environmental influence on the shot outcome is the wind. Mastering the wind is a skill that must be learned and is often overlooked. For this reason, I have included a chapter on taming the wind.

It is, of course, self-evident that a headwind can significantly reduce the shot distance while a tailwind will increase it. The player will use his experience before deciding on the club selection and club up or down accordingly.

Very strong headwinds or tailwinds of up to 30 mph can require clubbing up or down by three or four clubs.

When deciding on the type of shot to play, i.e., whether to shape it or not, the player should be mindful that it only takes a moderate crosswind of 5 mph to curve a straight shot or straighten a curved shot.

The player can use the wind to curve the shot by offsetting a straight shot towards the crosswind and 'riding' the wind.

A straight shot will rarely stay straight in a crosswind, even a moderate one. When it's windy, the player should expect the shot to curve. The key is to anticipate how it will curve before choosing the appropriate shot type.

The 'waggle' and the sightline and focal point adjustment are important parts of the setup for each shot, discussed briefly next.

THE CLUBHEAD LIFT AND WAGGLE

The waggle enables the player to obtain a feel for the club and the intended shot. It is perhaps the most important part of the setup. It is a release of tension that sets up the tempo of the swing.

First, the player obtains a feel for the combined heft of the arms and club by pushing down with the heel of the left hand to flex the wrist and lifting the clubhead vertically upwards a few inches above the ground. At the same time, the right forefinger and thumb are moved from the club to keep the grip and forearms free of tension, allowing the right elbow and shoulder joints to be activated.

The waggle to-and-fro should resemble the extended takeaway and follow-through. The clubhead travels on a shallow arc straight back and forwards above the target line for a short distance on either side of the ball, maintaining the clubface square to the target line for longer in the strike zone. Some players prefer to abbreviate the waggle, moving the clubhead straight back a short distance before returning it to the ball, ensuring the clubface is delivered square to the target line.

THE SIGHTLINE AND FOCAL POINT ADJUSTMENT

The sightline and focal point position for the normal stroke are established for each shot during the setup. Their purpose is to direct the vertical release direction of the clubhead into the follow-through while keeping the head still and the stroke stable.

Sightline and Focal Point Adjustment

Normal Stroke

SHOT-SHAPING

Some players shape the shot by opening or closing the clubface, others by changing their swing path, and others by changing their body alignment or stance.

When the baseline stroke is deployed, there is only one reliable way to shape the shot. The shot is shaped by purposefully adjusting the club and grip position during the setup to offset the clubface and clubshaft. Subsequently, the dynamic response of the baseline stroke to restore the club's balance is automatically harnessed to tilt the ball's spin axis and curve the shot. The stance adjusts naturally to provide an evenly balanced, stable base to the swing.

Regardless of the intended shape of the shot, the player maintains a 'connection' to the target line or intermediate target to guide the clubhead release and follow-through.

The clubhead is released automatically on the downswing; it is not steered or directed.

A shot made with a low lofted club or a lower shot is easier to curve because it has a lower spin rate. As a general rule, because a draw has less spin than the fade, it is easier to curve.

When deploying a baseline stroke, the player shouldn't expect massive draws or fades. In calm conditions, with a driver, the typical curve width will be five yards and slightly less for an iron.

To produce a wider curve on the shot, the player strengthens or weakens his right-hand grip to its maximum extent and makes a commensurate adjustment to his stance, starting the ball's flight further to the right or the left of the target.

DRAW SHOTS

To illustrate the setup process and shot execution, the low trajectory draw is described in the following images. As will be explained, a medium and higher trajectory draw is a variation of a low trajectory draw.

When presenting the clubface to the ball, the player carefully aims its leading edge towards an intermediate target on the ground, two or three feet ahead of the ball. At the same time, he tilts the clubshaft forwards slightly, orienting it to the target's right, promoting a draw. The right-hand grip is placed in a neutral position on the club for a low draw.

With the driver, to ensure the stance and the swing remain evenly balanced, the player may wish to introduce a small gap between the clubface and the ball when setting up for a draw.

The Low Draw – 6 Iron

A higher trajectory draw requires a strengthened right-hand grip with the clubshaft tilt positioned slightly forwards or neutral. Setting up with the ball positioned closer to the toe of the club will start the ball further right. The shot will curve more with a lower trajectory.

With a stronger right-hand grip, starting the downswing, there is a natural rearward tilting of the spine and closure of the shoulders. The right elbow is tucked under the body and moves closer to the right side above the hip as the shoulders close.

FADE SHOTS

To illustrate the setup process and shot execution, only the high fade is described in the following images. As will be explained, a lower fade is a variation of a high fade.

When presenting the clubface to the ball, the player carefully aims its leading edge toward an intermediate target. At the same time, he tilts the clubshaft to the rear slightly, orienting it to the target's left, promoting a fade.

The right-hand grip is placed in a neutral position on the club for a high fade.

A lower trajectory fade requires a weakened right-hand grip with the clubshaft tilt positioned to the rear or neutral. Setting up with the ball positioned closer to the heel of the club will start the ball further left. The shot will curve more with a lower trajectory.

The High Fade – 6 Iron

There is a natural change with a weaker right-hand grip, starting the downswing, reducing the spine's rearward tilt, and opening the shoulders slightly. The right elbow moves forwards to a position in front of the right side and hip as the shoulders open.

Having learned the keys to shot-shaping, the player can produce a straight shot that removes any potential for unwanted sidespin.

STRAIGHT SHOTS

Discounting wind, to produce a straight shot, the player has to remove any potential for inadvertently curving it. This is the reason I considered the shot-shaping segment first.

Any inadvertent shot curvature off-target is minimized by ensuring the right-hand grip is correctly matched to the left-hand grip as the clubshaft tilt is adjusted and by adopting the baseline stroke. Some players will match the left and right-hand grips before tilting the club forwards or to the rear. Other players prefer to adjust and position the right-hand grip to match it to the left-hand grip after tilting the club.

This section considers the setup process required to produce a straight shot of any trajectory, as shown in the following images. The stance adjusts naturally to provide an evenly balanced, stable base for the swing.

| The Low Straight Shot | The Medium Trajectory Straight Shot | The High Straight Shot |

A straight shot on target has very little spin axis tilt, finishing on or very close to the intended target line, let's say within ten yards on either side of it for a tee shot with a driver and half of that for an iron shot. There should be little or no deviation from the intended target line with a straight short iron shot. You will recall that a straight shot will curve in only a moderate crosswind.

THE LOW STRAIGHT SHOT

When presenting the clubface to the ball, the player carefully aims its leading edge toward an intermediate target. At the same time, he tilts the clubshaft forwards slightly. With the clubface aimed at the target, as the clubshaft is tilted forward, loft is removed from the clubface rotating the clubshaft to the left slightly. The player makes a corresponding adjustment to weaken the right-hand grip to match it with the left-hand grip.

With the driver, to ensure the swing remains evenly balanced, the player may wish to introduce a small gap between the clubface and the ball.

A low straight shot will typically involve an abbreviated 'sawn-off' finish with a short or medium iron. The player will continue into a high finish with a long shot, allowing the clubhead to release as normal. As a low shot requires less spin, the ball is compressed more.

The Low Straight Shot

THE MEDIUM TRAJECTORY STRAIGHT SHOT

The first of the following images shows a setup with no intentional tilt applied to the clubshaft and neutral, matching left and right-hand grips.

The left foot is naturally flared out a little to facilitate the clubhead's release toward the intermediate target. The right elbow and wrist are naturally flexed at impact to deliver the clubface square to the target line. The result is a powerful medium shot trajectory with no hint of a curve.

The Medium Trajectory Straight Shot

THE HIGH STRAIGHT SHOT

When presenting the clubface to the ball, the player carefully aims its leading edge toward an intermediate target. At the same time, he tilts the clubshaft to the rear slightly. With the clubface aimed at the target, as the clubshaft is tilted to the rear, loft is added to the clubface rotating the clubshaft to the right slightly. The player makes a corresponding adjustment to strengthen the right-hand grip to match it with the left hand. When the clubshaft is tilted to the rear, the stance and hips are naturally pivoted open more to keep the setup evenly balanced and provide unencumbered access for the stroke and clubhead release, along the target line, towards the intermediate target.

The High Straight Shot

The player's choice of a straight or curved tee shot will depend upon the wind speed and direction, the layout and slope of the fairway, and the hazards to be negotiated. Of course, some players will have a natural shape to their shots, which they might not want to change.

AVOIDING SPINAL INJURY

Certain situations require a curved shot from the tee. For example, when playing a links course where the fairways are extremely firm or overhanging trees block the target line. Depending on the wind, if an intentionally curved shot is not needed, the player might favor his natural shot shape or play for a straight shot.

The player should know that intentionally curving the shot in either direction may stress the spine. For example, a high draw shot with a driver may exert considerable stress on the lower lumbar spine, and a low fade shot with the driver may stress the upper part of the spine, the cervical spine.

There is little risk of twisting the spine when executing a straight shot of any trajectory. Hence there is less risk of spinal injury.

Several top players have suffered injuries to their spines early in their careers. Tiger Woods and Rory McIlroy began their careers with a preference for a high draw from the tee. Both have experienced lower back problems as a result. Other top players who suffered back problems were Fred Couples and Seve Ballesteros.

Faders of the ball tend to have less risk of spinal injury as their body weight is distributed forwards and is likely to be more centered at impact.

Ideally, players should spend at least twenty minutes on the driving range or in a hitting net to loosen up and stretch the muscles before playing.

Keeping the swing stable and evenly balanced, and modifying the swing speed accordingly, is essential to avoid back injury. Allowing a small space between the clubface and the ball is good when executing a draw with the driver. It helps to keep the swing stable and dynamically balanced.

CONCLUSION

The baseline stroke, anchored by the sightline and focal point, forms a solid foundation for every shot and unlocks the secrets of skilled shot-making with the precision and dynamism of the strike. The stroke is rehearsed with the clubhead lift and waggle.

With the baseline stroke, shot-shaping and direction control are essentially about how the player holds and positions the club and aims the clubface during the setup to balance the club and achieve the desired shot outcome.

It is a far simpler and more efficient approach than trying to swing the club in a prescribed manner by directing the swing path and manipulating the clubface. It avoids altogether the more complicated process of consciously adjusting and aligning the stance, the shoulders, and the ball position during the setup.

In the next chapter, with a range of long and short straight specialty shots, we consider how the spin rate and launch angle are changed to control the shot's trajectory and distance and determine how far the ball will roll on landing.

CHAPTER 5: ADVANCED SHOT-MAKING

The chapter explains and demonstrates the specialty golf shots that apply the blueprint for shot-making to control the spin rate, shot trajectory and distance, and the ball's behavior when it lands.

To aid a better understanding of the advanced shot-making outcomes, the shot data for each of the shots described in this chapter, together with ball flight profiles, are included in the Appendix at the end of the book. The data provides a powerful validation of the Shot-Maker's Code.

CHAPTER 5

ADVANCED SHOT-MAKING

In the last chapter, we demonstrated basic shot-making. In this chapter, the shots are a little more advanced. We will consider how we change the shot's launch angle and the spin rate to control its trajectory, carry distance, and the distance the ball will roll when it lands.

There are six specialty shot types to consider:

- The Power Spinner
- The Power Runner
- The Short Punch Shot
- The Running Pitch and Chip Shot
- The Laid-Back Cut Shot
- The Short Low Spinner

To execute any specialty shot, in addition to the two stroke variable adjustments described in the last chapter, only one further stroke adjustment is needed to add spin control to the player's repertoire of shot-making skills, his sightline and focal point.

The shots' launch data, ball flight profile, and downrange results are provided in the Appendix at the end of the book.

Sightline and Focal Point Adjustment

Laid-Back Cut Stroke *Power Stroke*

→ To Target

THE POWER SHOT

The power shot is associated with a full shot made with any club. The term 'power' is descriptive of the energy imparted to the ball and the resultant ball flight. Relative to the slope of the ground, when the baseline stroke is extended, and the club and clubhead are released more forward than down into the follow-through, the ball is compressed more on the clubface for longer. As a consequence, the ball will hold its line for longer on a powerful penetrating mid-trajectory and can be controlled to stop quickly or roll on landing.

The power stroke extends the baseline stroke maximizing the width of the swing arc. It is a very efficient and effective stroke, as more of the kinetic energy produced by the motion of the downward and forward swing is conserved to drive the ball forward. As long as the baseline stroke is deployed, the power stroke can be applied to a straight shot or a curved shot.

When a power shot is deployed, the player has the option of stopping the ball quickly when it lands or allowing it to roll some distance by using the forward stroke to dynamically add loft to the clubface or reduce it when the clubhead is released. As the clubface loft is added or reduced during impact itself, the clubhead is stable, and the clubface is kept square to the target line for longer. The risk of inadvertently manually opening or closing the clubface and producing a wayward shot is less.

THE POWER SPINNER

The power spinner is normally used for an approach shot with an iron, but it can be used with any club as long as the lie is good, even from fairway bunkers. It utilizes the forward stroke to dynamically add loft to increase the ball's launch angle and stop it quickly on landing. It can also be used with the driver when the player wishes to curtail any run on the ball. The ball's stopping power is ideal for negotiating tight fairways from the tee to avoid hazards and thick rough.

Due to the higher launch angle, the ball rises steeply at the start of its flight. The near-horizontal strike forward and the low spin rate prevents the ball from flying high and losing distance. At the end of its flight, the ball drops steeply, with little, if any, roll on landing. It is also commonly known as a knockdown shot in today's parlance. The term spinner denotes the shot's ability to hold onto its spin rate for longer and stop the ball quickly on landing.

To execute the power spinner, the player sets up for a low straight shot, deploying forward tilt on the clubshaft and a weak right-hand grip. He directs his gaze to the back of the ball, the point on the ball farthest from the target. The player's sightline and focal point for the power stroke is referenced in the graphic shown earlier in the chapter.

The idea is to promote a more horizontal, forward release of the clubhead parallel to the ball's equator. In reality, as the club has loft, the ball will always be struck below its equator unless it is topped.

For the power spinner, the adjustment to the sightline positions the ball slightly further forward in the stance than would normally be the case for a low-trajectory straight shot. The stance naturally adjusts to allow the player access to extend the release of the club and clubhead horizontally forward toward the target. The player focuses on striking the back of the ball and releasing the clubhead on a shallow arc along the target line in the strike zone.

The Power Spinner: 6-Iron

A less-than-full power spinner with a 'sawn-off' finish is usually referred to as a punch shot, covered later in the chapter.

THE POWER RUNNER

The power runner is used exclusively with the driver and other long clubs from the tee or on a long par 5. Its purpose is to maximize the amount of roll and the overall shot distance. It utilizes the forward stroke to dynamically remove loft to reduce the ball's launch angle. As the ball is flighted lower, it will roll more on landing.

It is the best shot to play from the tee in windy conditions; the low spin rate keeps the ball down and reduces its flight time, thereby minimizing the risk of a wayward shot. The shot is also ideal to use on wide, firm fairways where the ball can run.

To execute the power runner, the player sets up for a high straight shot, deploying rearward tilt on the clubshaft and a strong right-hand grip. He directs his gaze to the back of the ball, the point on the ball farthest from the target.

The stance adjusts naturally to allow the player access to extend the release of the club and clubhead horizontally forward toward the target.

An abbreviated version of the power runner stroke, commonly known as the stinger, will further reduce the launch angle and landing angle to further increase the distance the ball rolls when it lands. The stinger is an ideal tee shot to play onto a downslope or where the fairway is firm and will accept more roll.

The Power Runner: Driver

As a general principle, the spin rate is minimized on tee shots to obtain a powerful, penetrating ball flight and to maximize the shot's overall distance, accuracy, and control.

As you might expect, the stable clubhead in the strike zone significantly improves the shot's reliability, distance control, and accuracy. For this reason, many top players consider the power runner with the driver to be the most valuable and reliable shot in golf; see the following images.

The Power Runner: Driver
The Extent of a Square Clubface through the Impact Zone

With a more stable clubhead obtained in the strike zone, the player significantly reduces the scope for a wayward shot.

The fundamentals that apply to the power spinner also apply to the short punch shot.

THE SHORT PUNCH SHOT WITH A 56° SAND WEDGE

The short, sawn-off, low trajectory punch shot played with a sand wedge or a lob wedge, or indeed even a longer iron, is a perfect shot for finding a pin positioned at the front of the green or for controlling the ball on a green sloping away from the player.

A shot landing just short of the green on the front fringe will stop quickly on the green on its second or third bounce. This shot is not appropriate if the fairway is wet, as the ball may stick in the fringe.

To execute the shot, the player sets up with the clubshaft tilted forward and a weak right-hand grip. He tilts his head to the side to sight the back of the ball. His focus is on striking down firmly and releasing the club and clubhead forward into the follow-through.

The Short Punch Shot: 56° Sand Wedge

The fundamentals that apply to the power runner with the driver also apply to a running pitch shot or a running chip shot.

THE RUNNING PITCH AND CHIP SHOT WITH A 52° GAP WEDGE

Rolling the ball is an option when the hole is at the back of the green or the green is sloped from back to front.

Distance control is easier on short pitches and chips when the ball is flighted lower and rolling more. The likelihood of the ball dropping into the cup as the ball rolls forward is increased. A gap wedge is appropriate for this shot as the player wants the right balance of spin and roll.

The clubshaft is tilted back slightly or set in a neutral, upright position, and the right-hand grip is strengthened slightly during the setup. To enhance his feel for the stroke and strike, the player grips down on the club, which moves his stance slightly closer to the ball.

Gripping down on the club will produce a shorter, abbreviated stroke, less wrist flex, and will further reduce the launch angle and landing angle, creating less spin and increasing the distance the ball rolls when it lands.

The clubhead is released forward, using 'touch and feel' to gauge the shot height and distance and how far the ball will roll forward on the green. An abbreviated pitching stroke will reduce the shot trajectory and create more roll. A lengthened pitching stroke will produce more height on the shot, rolling the ball less.

A shortened stroke, akin to a putting stroke, is appropriate for running a chip shot, flighting the ball lower, and producing more roll. For a longer running chip shot, a lower lofted club may be used.

The Running Pitch Shot: 52° Gap Wedge

The same principles apply to the putting stroke. A putter held upright with a slightly stronger right-hand grip will keep the putter face square to the aim point for longer, start the ball rolling sooner, and improve the player's 'feel' for the roll and distance of the putt.

THE SHORT, LAID-BACK CUT SHOT WITH A 60° LOB WEDGE

The term 'cut' usually denotes a fade to most golfers. This section describes a straight short, laid-back cut stroke. It refers to a steep underarm stroke with a laid-back clubface delivered square to the target line. A cut shot is any stroke using vertical hinging of the left shoulder and wrist joints. It will have less roll and more 'bite'.

While the laid-back cut shot can be deployed with longer irons, for the purposes of this demonstration, a short shot with a 60-degree lob wedge is described.

The shot is deployed on approach shots, typically of 80 yards or less, when the player wants to maximize the spin rate and conserve it in the ball to stop it quickly on landing. It is normally a straight shot, not a fade, and normally associated with a lower trajectory wedge shot.

The player progressively pivots the stance more open for shots closer to the hole.

When executing a short, laid-back cut shot, as a general rule, a weaker right-hand grip will help to flight the ball lower and stop the ball quickly when it lands.

To execute the short laid-back cut shot with a wedge, imagine that the swing plane is no longer inclined; it is upright. The player tilts the club forward, so it is resting on its wide sole and weakens his right-hand grip before placing it on the club. His sightline is directed towards a point on the top of the ball, and his strike intent is to steepen the downward direction of release of the clubhead and lay back the clubface with an underarm stroke. The player's sightline and focal point for the laid-back cut stroke is referenced in the graphic earlier in the chapter.

He moves the club back and up with the arms and shoulders, keeping the clubhead moving back and higher above the ball-to-target line's rearward extension and pointing the toe of the clubhead upwards.

The player follows the reverse path on the forward swing, striking down firmly into the ground under the ball with the wide sole of the club with the clubface laid-back. There is little, if any, forward motion of the ball when it lands as it is still spinning back.

The Short Laid-Back Cut Shot: 60° Lob Wedge

To increase the amount of clubface lay-back at impact and increase and conserve more of the spin rate when wanting to spin the ball backward or to the side on a slope when it lands on the green. Keeping most of his weight on his left side, the player opens the clubface and weakens his right-hand grip further; he strikes down firmly into the ground under the ball.

A stronger right-hand grip or slower swing speed is needed to allow the ball to roll forward when it lands, which reduces the magnitude of the strike. An abbreviated sawn-off finish will produce less spin when hitting against a strong headwind and prevent the ball from ballooning.

Adjusting the right-hand grip strength to control how far the ball rolls on the green is useful when playing out of a greenside bunker. With a laid-back cut shot, a weaker right-hand grip will stop the ball quickly, and a stronger right-hand grip will allow it to roll some distance. A laid-back cut shot is also useful for extricating the ball from thick rough as it will reduce the risk of long grass entangling around the club's hosel.

Maximizing and conserving spin with a laid-back cut shot requires a good sense of touch and feel to deliver a solid strike.

Unless the shot is very short, the hands and wrists should remain relatively 'quiet' on the backswing, with the club being held up mainly with the back, shoulders, and forearms, not with the hands. Consequently, all four main muscle groups drive the swing and the strike, delivering more energy to the ball. The hands and arms automatically firm up in the hitting area to deliver a solid, crisp strike.

The short, laid-back cut shot is shaped to influence the direction the ball will roll when it lands. When the conserved spin rate is maximized, rotating the hips more on the backswing will cause the ball to spin back to the right on a level green. Rotating them more on the downswing will cause the ball to spin back to the left.

THE LOW SPINNER

The short, low-trajectory wedge shot, otherwise more commonly known as the low spinner, is a mini version of the short, laid-back cut shot used for distances of 30 yards or less. The low spinner has less spin imparted on the ball than the longer version of the shot to keep the ball flight low. Its name derives from the fact that the ball is still spinning when it lands on the green, allowing it to slow its progress and stop within a short distance after the second bounce, typically within a few yards after landing.

The low spinner is very effective when played from hard turf, typical of a seaside links course. It is also a favored shot of tour and college players in America, where the greens tend to be firm and undulating.

Sighting the top of the ball, the player tilts the clubshaft forward to promote a low shot trajectory. A weak right-hand grip promotes a more vertical wrist hinge and maximum clubface lay-back to maximize the spin rate with a firm downward strike below the ball.

The 30-Yard Low Spinner: 60° Lob Wedge

On shots of less than 30 yards, the clubface must be allowed to pivot open on the club's wide sole to reduce the shot distance.

Any moisture on the green from rain or dew will make the ball skid more on the first bounce, delaying the spin from taking effect. If very wet, it may take two or three bounces before stopping on the fourth bounce. On softer greens, most, if not all, of the backspin degrades on the first bounce due to the higher friction force of the soft turf acting on the ball.

If the ball spins on a sloping green, it will spin back or to the side to follow the slope's direction. The player can anticipate this by choosing the appropriate landing point on the green. The turf's grain, firmness, and moisture presence will also influence how the ball spins and rolls on the green.

A lob shot or flop shot is a variation of a laid-back cut shot. It is a loose-wristed pitch in which the club is taken up abruptly on the backswing and dropped down steeply, sliding the clubface under the ball. As the clubface passes under the ball, the spin rate is very low as there is very little traction. The ball ascends almost vertically upwards, falls back to the green, and stops dead.

SHAPING A POWER SHOT AND A LAID-BACK CUT SHOT

Providing the baseline stroke is used, the player can shape either variant of the straight power shot by sighting the back of the ball and pivoting the stance and hips, and releasing the clubhead normally toward the target.

When the power runner is adapted to fade the shot, the stance and hips are pivoted counter-clockwise into a more open position than normally applied with the straight power runner. Otherwise, the shot is unchanged.

Shaping a Power Runner: Fade

For a draw, the power spinner is used. The pivot of the stance is rotated clockwise from its normally open position into an almost square or slightly closed position.

There is only a marginal difference in the overall shot distance between the power draw, the power fade, and the power straight shot.

Shaping a Power Spinner: Draw

Both shots produce a powerful mid-trajectory ball flight, providing the player with more control of the shot, especially when it's windy.

An alternative way to produce a mid-trajectory power fade or power draw without the need for an intentional stance adjustment is to incorporate a forward power stroke to the low fade or the high draw shots, described in the last chapter.

The player shapes the shorter laid-back cut shot by altering his hip alignment and rotation to change the ball's start line.

Shaping a Short Laid-Back Cut Shot

Because of a higher spin rate, a short, laid-back cut shot is more difficult to fade than to draw.

It will tend to spin back when it lands on the green and roll in the slope's direction. A laid-back cut shot curved from right to left will have less backspin. The skilled shot-maker takes account of this when choosing where to land the ball on the green.

SUMMARY

The power shots and the short, laid-back cut shot change the ball's launch conditions in a controlled way, utilizing the strike's precision, dynamics, and efficiency. An essential prerequisite for using a specialty shot is correctly executing the baseline stroke and allowing the clubhead to release naturally into the follow-through.

The power runner is ideal with a driver from the tee and for use with other long clubs; it maximizes roll and distance on the long shot and optimizes its accuracy and distance with a powerful and stable strike. The power spinner is more suited to iron approach shots to help the ball stop quickly when it lands.

When a power shot is used, extending the baseline stroke, it can be curved in either direction without an undue loss of distance.

The shorter laid-back cut stroke has a steeper downward clubhead release. It reduces the shot trajectory and flight time and maximizes and conserves spin on short approach shots to control the ball's behavior when it lands. It is also used from a greenside bunker to extricate the ball from the sand and control how far it rolls when it lands on the green.

A short or long punch shot may be used to stop the ball close to a hole positioned on the front of the green. When the hole is positioned closer to the back of the green, the running pitch or chip shot is often the player's choice of shot to increase the likelihood of holing it.

CONCLUSION

The hallmark of a good ball-striker and shot-maker is a player who can keep the spin rate and ball flight stable, optimizing the shot distance and judging how far to roll the ball when it lands.

The shot-maker will possess the essential tools to produce any shot outcome with a high degree of confidence, control, and precision. The player relies upon sensory feedback and 'feel' to guide the stroke and strike.

His confidence and belief are significantly enhanced when he controls the golf shot. Golf then becomes a challenge for him to master, and he will seek every opportunity to do so, adding to his self-esteem and prowess as a master ball-striker and shot-maker.

The next chapter considers how the shot-maker's control of the ball is the key to combatting and harnessing the wind.

CHAPTER 6: TAMING THE WIND

The chapter explores perhaps the most underrated skill in golf, wind play.

The effect of wind on the ball flight is illustrated with launch data. It demonstrates the importance of spin control and a stable ball flight in combatting or harnessing the wind.

CHAPTER 6

TAMING THE WIND

The key to playing well in the wind is understanding how the wind will affect the ball's flight and knowing what is needed to counteract it or harness it to produce the desired shot outcome. Wind play is probably one of the most underrated skills in golf. An essential requirement for combatting the wind is the player's ability to control the ball's launch angle, direction, spin rate, and spin axis.

When faced with strong winds, the sensible player adjusts his playing strategy to flight the ball lower against a headwind and higher against a tailwind with the choice of club and stroke. He offsets the target appropriately when faced with a direct or indirect crosswind.

The effect of the wind on the flight of the ball is greater at high wind speeds. In a direct crosswind, the effect of the wind on the shot is significant even at moderately low wind speeds.

The player's ball-striking and shot-making skills are an essential element of his armory in combatting or harnessing the wind. This chapter explains how the wind affects the ball's flight and highlights the hazards of a high spin rate with a driver shot in calm and windy conditions. It explains how a mastery of shot-making can be hugely beneficial in combatting the wind.

The analysis of the effect of wind on actual shot data in this chapter has been made possible by the OptimalFlight Analysis Tool and the Trackman Launch Monitor.

THE EFFECT OF WIND ON THE BALL FLIGHT

The wind's effect on the ball's flight is influenced significantly by its speed and direction. A strong headwind will increase the airflow velocity around the ball and cause it to hold onto its spin for longer.

These two factors increase aerodynamic lift and drag, potentially causing the ball to 'balloon' upwards and 'stall,' ultimately losing distance. The higher the spin rate, ball speed, and wind speed, the greater the potential for ballooning. Similarly, the ball's airflow velocity will also increase the sidespin force and cause it to hold onto any sidespin for longer. The player must launch the shot lower to reduce lift and drag.

The opposite is the case in a tailwind; the reduced airflow around the ball causes the spin rate to decay more rapidly and forces it lower in its flight. At a certain point, it can 'dip down' to the ground and run, like a hare, on landing. The player needs to launch the ball higher to counter the drop in the aerodynamic lift.

A crosswind does not have any significant effect on the ball's aerodynamics. However, it can 'push' the ball a considerable distance off-line, especially on a high ball flight. A compounding crosswind can be extremely damaging if the player mistimes the shot and produces a hook or a slice.

HEADWINDS AND TAILWINDS

When considering an appropriate shot to combat a headwind or a tailwind, there are two obvious questions to answer:

1. How will it affect the shot distance, both carry distance and roll?
2. How will it affect the curve width and off-target distance?

Let's answer each question with some examples of actual shot data.

Table 1 shows the effect of headwinds and tailwinds on the same drive. The total shot distance steadily increases as the headwind's speed drops and the tailwind's speed increases.

A strong headwind can significantly reduce the overall shot distance. In a 30 mph headwind, a ball hit by a driver can lose over 80 yards of the total distance expected in no wind. The ball will stop when it lands.

The increase in the carry distance of a drive down a tailwind is significant. However, it will not increase indefinitely with an increasingly stronger tailwind because the lift reduction tends to cancel out the drag reduction.

At very high wind speeds of over 30 mph, the rate of increase of the carry distance will gradually drop as the wind speed increases in a tailwind. The more significant effect of a strong tailwind is the increase in roll and the overall shot distance.

Table 1: The Effect of a Headwind and Tailwind on a Medium Trajectory Straight Drive

Wind Speed MPH	Carry Distance Yards	Roll Distance Yards	Total Distance Yards
30 (against)	234.4	0.0	234.4
20 (against)	257.4	4.2	261.5
10 (against)	277.4	12.8	290.2
Calm	294.3	22.9	317.2
10 (behind)	308.2	36.3	344.5
20 (behind)	319.0	51.7	370.6
30 (behind)	326.8	66.9	393.6

Data Sources: Trackman Launch Monitor and OptimalFlight Analysis Tool

The effects of a 20 mph headwind and tailwind on a straight drive are shown in the next graphic. Note the significant difference in the carry and roll distances affecting the shot. The other major difference is the height of the shot. Compared to a shot with no wind, the headwind shot was five yards higher, and the tailwind shot was five yards lower.

How a Headwind and Tailwind Affect a Medium Trajectory Drive

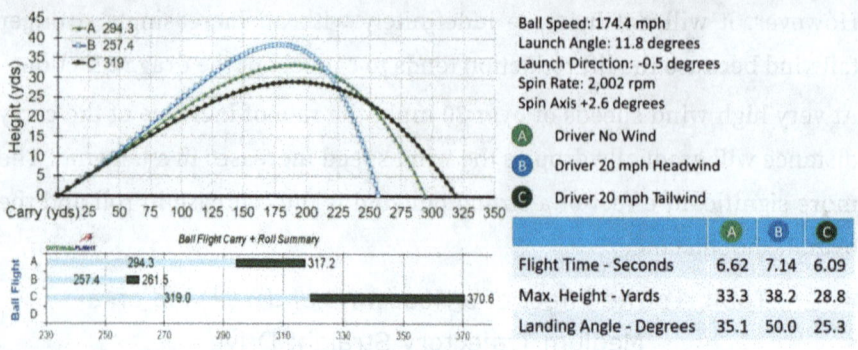

Data Sources: Trackman Launch Monitor and OptimalFlight Analysis Tool
(Air Temp: 70 Degrees F, Altitude: Sea Level, Standard Fairway Hardness)

A strong headwind is potentially damaging in reducing the shot's distance. It has even more damaging consequences on any unwanted sidespin. It can potentially double a hook's or slice's width in terms of off-target side distance when the ball lands.

A hooked drive into a 30 mph headwind will be more than twice the width of the same shot played down a 30 mph tailwind. There are two reasons for this. Firstly, the amount a ball with sidespin will curve in the air is proportional to the square of the time the sidespin force operates. Secondly, the hooking or slicing force acting on the ball will vary depending on the airflow speed, just as the lift force does.

The length of time the ball remains airborne will vary according to the strength of the wind blowing behind or against it; see Table 2. Because a drive into a headwind remains in the air longer than a drive downwind, a hooked drive into a 30 mph headwind would potentially be nearly twice as crooked as the same shot hit downwind due to the difference in flight time alone.

The sidespin force produced by a hooked drive into a 30 mph headwind is nearly one and a half times that of the sidespin force from a hooked drive with the same wind speed from behind.

Bringing the two factors of sidespin force and the time of flight together, any hooked or sliced drive in a strong headwind is likely to have a curve width of over twice that of the same shot down a strong tailwind.

Note the effect of a headwind and tailwind on the shot's side deviation. The shot is significantly more wayward into the wind than downwind.

Table 2: The Effect of a Headwind/Tailwind on a Hooked Drive

Wind Speed MPH	Carry Distance Yards	Total Distance Yards	Curve Width Yards	Side Carry Yards	Time of Flight Seconds
30 (against)	223.5	224.3	13.4	-22.2	6.77
20 (against)	243.1	249.7	11.5	-18.5	6.52
10 (against)	259.8	275.9	10.0	-15.0	6.27
Calm	273.7	300.6	8.7	-11.5	6.02
10 (behind)	284.6	325.7	7.6	-8.2	5.76
20 (behind)	292.7	348.0	6.7	-5.0	5.5
30 (behind)	298.1	370.5	5.8	-2.1	5.25

Data Sources: Trackman Launch Monitor and OptimalFlight Analysis Tool

The following graphic shows how a strong headwind and tailwind affect a hook.

There is a significant variation in the carry distance, the amount of roll, and each shot's overall distance.

Notice how the hook straightens when launched down a strong tailwind and curves more when played into a strong headwind.

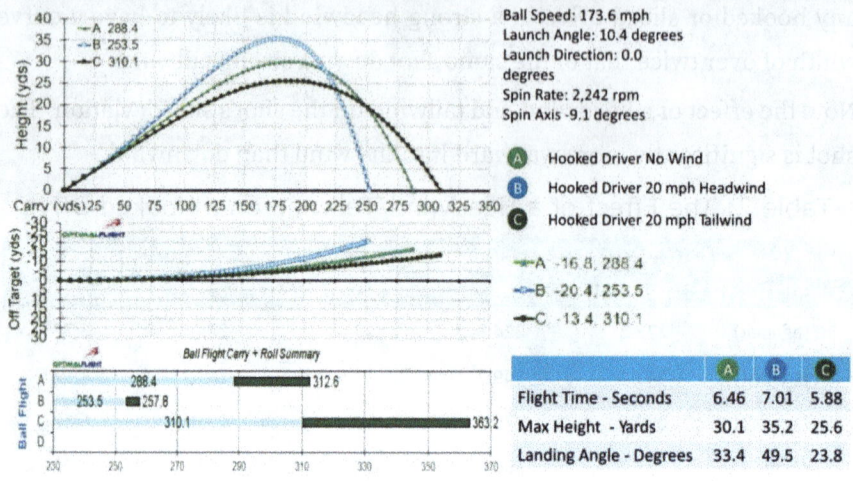

Data Sources: Trackman Launch Monitor and OptimalFlight Analysis Tool
(Air Temp: 70 Degrees F, Altitude: Sea Level, Standard Fairway Hardness)

The effect of a strong headwind is more significant with shorter clubs because of the higher launch angle and higher spin rate. A hooked short iron into a 30 mph headwind would travel sideways one yard for every two yards of travel forwards.

CROSSWINDS

A crosswind has only a marginal effect on the shot's height or distance. The more important effect of a crosswind is its ability to move the ball sideways a considerable distance. Table 3 shows the effect of a direct crosswind on a medium trajectory straight shot made with a selection of clubs.

The wind actually pushes the ball sideways, which may progressively increase as the ball flies higher, where it might be more exposed to the wind; this is even more likely at high elevations on the course. The effect of a strong crosswind is also more significant when the fairway is not tree-lined, e.g., on a seaside links course.

Table 3: The Effect of a Crosswind on a Normal Straight Shot

Club	Carry Distance Yards	10 mph Crosswind		20 mph Crosswind		30 mph Crosswind	
		Side Deviation from Target Yards	Increase/Decrease in Carry Distance Yards	Side Deviation from Target Yards	Increase/Decrease in Carry Distance Yards	Side Deviation from Target Yards	Increase/Decrease in Carry Distance Yards
1W	284	14.3	+2	21.5	+2	43.1	+1
3I	226	16.3	Nil	32.0	Nil	49.3	-1
6I	183	16.3	Nil	32.7	-1	49.3	-2
8I	161	16.8	Nil	32.7	-1	49.0	-2
PW	138	14.0	Nil	28.1	-1	42.7	-3

Data Sources: Trackman Launch Monitor and OptimalFlight Analysis Tool

Its effect on a straight shot depends on its launch characteristics, i.e., launch angle, spin rate, and ball speed. A moderate crosswind will turn a straight shot into a curved shot.

Up to a certain point, a higher launch angle will obtain more distance on the shot, and because it remains in the air for longer, it will also carry sideways farther.

The target offset distance needed to counter a direct crosswind will vary depending on the shot's trajectory. The higher the shot trajectory, the more target offset is needed.

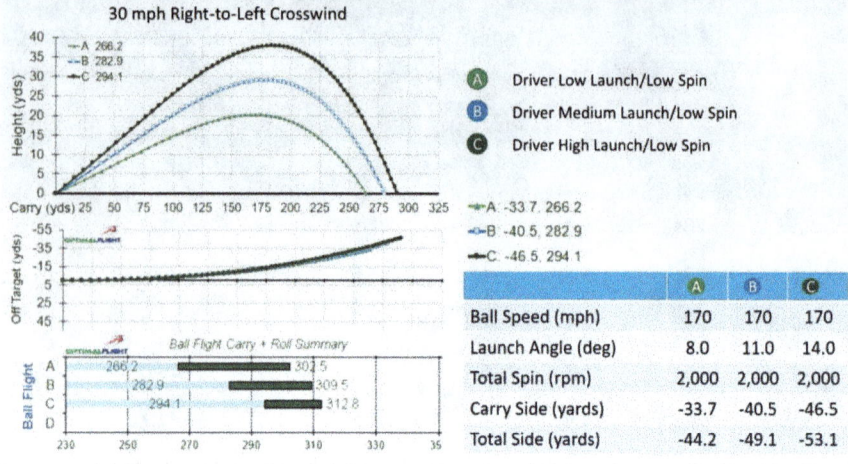

Data Source: Trackman Launch Monitor and OptimalFlight Analysis Tool
(Air Temp: 70 Degrees F, Altitude: Sea Level, Standard Fairway Hardness)

THE EFFECTS OF THE WIND ON EXCESSIVE DRIVER SPIN

Wayward shots are commonplace with the driver and other deep-faced clubs, particularly when a strong wind blows and the spin rate is too low or high.

When the ball is hooked or sliced, excessive spin is perhaps one of the main factors responsible for big misses and shots sailing out of bounds. Excessive spin means that the ball will stay airborne for longer, increasing the height and the curve width of a wayward shot. The player who knows how to keep the spin rate stable is best equipped to deal with this often-unseen hazard.

Many players do not realize that the spin generated can vary significantly with the longer clubs. For example, a driver's spin rate can be as low as 1,000 rpm or 3,000 rpm or higher. The optimal spin rate for a stable ball flight optimizing the shot's distance and accuracy will depend on the player's clubhead speed.

The more skilled player typically has a driver spin rate of 2,000 rpm or slightly higher; a lesser skilled player will have a lower clubhead speed and a higher spin rate.

The main cause of excessive spin with the driver is hitting the ball too hard and steeply without releasing the clubhead forwards, adding loft to the clubface. A steep, firm descending strike with the driver or fairway wood is potentially hazardous as it can increase the spin rate and produce a damaging high slice.

Excessive driver spin can be highly dangerous when confronted with a strong headwind or a crosswind. Against a strong headwind, it can curve the ball upwards steeply, as alluded to earlier, and risks the shot ballooning out of control and falling significantly short.

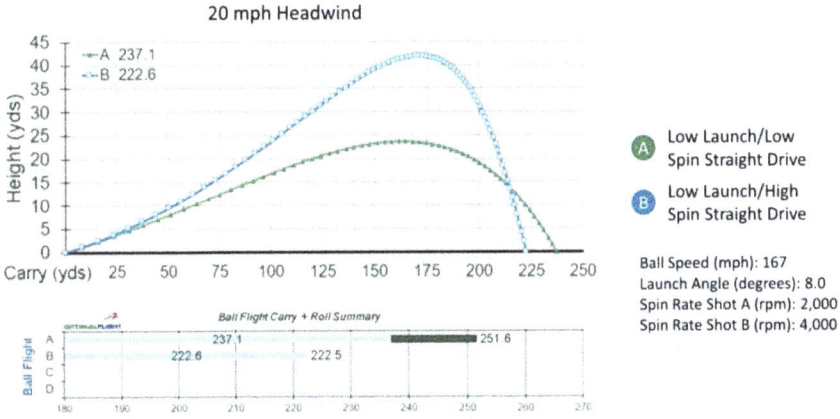

Data Source: Trackman Launch Monitor and OptimalFlight Analysis Tool
(Air Temp: 70 Degrees F, Altitude: Sea Level, Standard Fairway Hardness)

In a strong crosswind, an increase in spin rate of just 1,000 rpm will increase the distance off-line by nearly a half and lose distance on the shot.

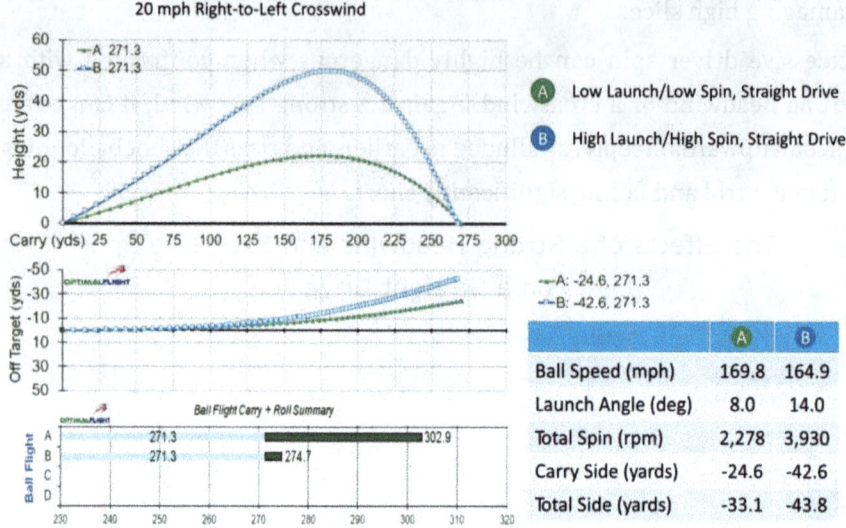

Data Sources: Trackman Launch Monitor and OptimalFlight Analysis Tool
(Air Temp: 70 Degrees F, Altitude: Sea Level, Standard Fairway Hardness)

Given that it doesn't take a very strong crosswind to produce a big miss with the driver, the player's clear priority is to balance the spin rate and launch angle to keep the ball flight low but stable.

The skilled player's ability to create a spin rate that is neither too high nor too low when driving in windy conditions is an important factor that marks him out as a skilled ball-striker.

COMBATTING AND HARNESSING THE WIND

Against a strong headwind or tailwind, the player should club up by choosing a lower-lofted club or club down by choosing a higher-lofted club. In very strong headwinds or tailwinds, with speeds of more than 20 mph, the player should typically club up or down by three clubs or more.

A low straight shot is desirable when faced with a strong headwind. When choosing a longer club, the stroke is abbreviated to reduce the shot distance if required by choking down with the grip. A powerful mid-trajectory power runner shot is ideal when the wind blows strongly from the side or behind.

The shot will hold its line for longer and is less susceptible to potentially harmful sidespin.

On short approach shots to the green, the player strikes the ball firmly to hold onto the spin rate and stop the ball quickly on landing when faced with a strong tailwind. When faced with a strong headwind, to prevent the ball from ballooning, he reduces the magnitude of the strike and allows the ball to run.

The target line and setup alignment are offset towards the wind to combat a direct or indirect crosswind. The player executes a straight low or mid-trajectory shot, allowing the wind to curve the shot toward the target. The amount of offset will vary depending on the wind speed and direction, the club and shot selection, and the shot trajectory. It will typically range from one to one and a half yards of offset adjustment for every one mph of crosswind speed.

Experienced players can gauge the wind speed very accurately by observing its effects. In a 15 mph wind, leaves and small twigs are in constant motion. Small trees sway at a wind speed of 20 mph, and crested wavelets form on a water surface. At 30 mph, large trees will be moving.

At speeds higher than 30 mph, the wind will whistle against a steel clubshaft, and the ball will move on the green.

CONCLUSION

When faced with strong headwinds, the obvious conclusion is to select a longer club, as a lower spin rate and faster ball speed help the ball penetrate the wind. When selecting the driver or any other wood when it's windy, the player must be aware of the extreme hazards of an excessively high or low spin rate.

The optimum full shot for playing in the wind with any club is a low or mid-trajectory shot, regardless of the wind direction.

When the wind is blowing hard, the efficiency of the stroke and strike is what matters. A stable and well-balanced swing is a key ingredient for effective wind play. To maintain the dynamic balance of the swing, the player will intuitively adjust his stance, posture, and swing speed, swinging neither too fast nor too slow.

In the next chapter, we take a deep dive to examine the modern golf swing and stroke. Remember, the swing is a natural and intuitive response to how the player configures the stroke during the setup. Hence, the swing, or elements of it, must never be viewed in isolation but as part of the stroke that created it.

CHAPTER 7: THE MODERN GOLF SWING

A comprehensive analysis and demonstration of the modern golf swing and stroke pioneered by Ben Hogan.

The chapter contains the swing sequence as well as an introduction to the automated conical pendulum release and how it helps in sustaining clubhead lag.

The chapter stresses the role of the hands in the modern golf swing and the importance of dynamic balance in motion, rhythm, and an even tempo. The role of sensory awareness and feedback in seeing and feeling the shot is also explored.

CHAPTER 7

THE MODERN GOLF SWING

This chapter departs from the relatively straightforward narrative of previous chapters. It contains a detailed description of the modern golf swing and stroke using technical terms that are possibly unfamiliar to many readers. Please refer to the Glossary at the end of the book to define the terms used.

An automated modern golf swing and stroke is a natural consequence of configuring and applying The Shot-Maker's Code.

This chapter describes the modern swing in detail to help the reader understand how it automatically reacts to what has gone before. The swing is a natural and intuitive response to configuring the stroke during the setup. When the player understands this, he can avoid potentially damaging swing changes. Having learned the stroke for the shot, he must put complete trust and faith in his swing.

Today's modern swing can be likened to a high-performance car. While a comfortable ride, the traditional hands and arms swing leaves a lot in the tank. The modern body swing is less elegant and graceful than its predecessor but more powerful.

We have the equipment manufacturers to thank for the evolution of the traditional swing into a modern, powerful, athletic golf swing and stroke. A very important milestone was reached in 1935 with the invention of the new machine-wound high inertia Titleist ball with its hard vulcanized rubber core and cover.

Once again, after a hiatus of more than thirty years, the skilled player could control the ball and determine its flight with greater precision.

The Titleist ball led to advances in club technology towards more resilient, lighter, and longer clubs. It demanded a powerful precision golf stroke, which necessitated a much more powerful and compact swing, creating more width than depth. Suddenly our cherished game of golf, a pastime enjoyed by millions of enthusiasts worldwide, became a highly competitive global international sport. It was brought into our living rooms in glorious technicolor in 1962 by NBC from the beautiful island of Hawaii. Golf fans in the U.K. had to wait until 1967 to enjoy the color revolution in viewing tournament golf on television.

Now we can identify the fundamentals of today's modern athletic swing in some detail. As described and demonstrated in this chapter, the swing looks remarkably similar to the one documented by Mr. Hogan in his acclaimed book, The Modern Fundamentals of Golf, 1957. It doesn't stop here, though; the swing is a work in progress.

As the swing naturally evolves from the golf stroke, it will continue to evolve as stronger players inject more power into the stroke, helped by further advances in equipment technology. Some of today's top players, who might occasionally be seen struggling to keep the ball on the fairway with their prodigious distances from the tee, will potentially be the pioneers of the future post-modern swing. They will fashion a stroke and swing that will become more familiar to television viewers in the decades to come. One that perhaps will look very different from the swing shape we are familiar with today.

THE TRADITIONAL SWING

The traditional swing is still taught today and has been used very successfully by some of the world's greatest players, including Sam Snead and Jack Nicklaus. It has width and depth in equal proportion.

It starts with a one-piece takeaway, with the hips, shoulders, and arms all turning back together. To facilitate the hip pivot, the left heel is lifted off the ground exerting pressure on the ball of the foot. As the pelvis pivots clockwise on the backswing, the torso and shoulders sit on top of the pelvis and go along for the ride. The arms are swung back together.

A short lateral takeaway is incorporated into the swing with the aid of a forward press. A conscious effort is needed to extend the release of the clubhead and incorporate a follow-through of similar length after impact.

Shots are shaped by altering the swing path to change the ball's initial line of flight relative to the intended target.

CHARACTERISTICS OF THE MODERN SWING

Today's shorter and more compact swing, pioneered by Ben Hogan, is mechanically more efficient than its predecessors possessing more width than depth. Assisted by an extended takeaway, it maximizes potential muscular energy on the backswing to power the stroke.

Unlike the traditional swing that is leveraged mainly by the cocking and uncocking of the wrists, the modern stroke is leveraged by the transfer of weight down and into the left side on the downswing, activating the powerful leg, hip, and glute muscles.

To accommodate more power, it is vitally important that the swing remains firmly planted, stable, and evenly balanced in all directions from start to finish.

The clubhead leads the hands on the extended takeaway to allow the player's weight to move over the right hip joint before starting the uplift. On the forward swing, the sequence is reversed to move the player's weight over the left hip joint before releasing the clubhead into the follow-through.

The swing, when executed correctly, is a full-body swing from the outset. It engages all of the body's four main muscle groups early in the backswing to maximize centripetal acceleration and efficiently transmit kinetic energy to the clubhead and ball. The body swings the arms and club together.

The modern swing is an automatic, reflexive response to the stroke as configured and the extended takeaway and follow-through. The player must allow the senses to control the execution of the swing without any external intervention. The swing is guided by sight, perception, touch, and feel; the player must 'see and feel' the shot. When the stroke has been configured correctly, the swing is automated, requiring no manual interference from the player.

In the modern swing, the dominant right arm and shoulder control the arms' and club's vertical up-and-down motion and the body's rotation. The left arm and shoulder have a largely passive and reactive role.

SEQUENCING THE MODERN SWING

A solid, precision golf stroke and strike that maximizes compression requires an optimized, mechanically efficient motion. The modern, athletic swing fulfills that requirement.

In the modern swing, we can identify six movements that merge into one seamless, continuous, flowing, rhythmical motion:

1. The Extended Takeaway
2. The Upswing
3. The Transition
4. The Start Down
5. The Extended Release and Follow-Through
6. The Finish

The swing is broken down into different parts to help explain it better. It is important to note that the swing is an unconsciously controlled effort with a continuous flow once the takeaway has ended.

The extended takeaway and clubhead release into the follow-through are two 'bookends' providing the swing with the stability to maintain its dynamic balance, essential for reliable shot-making.

In demonstrating the swing sequence, the player has set up to execute a medium trajectory straight shot with neutral, matching left and right-hand grips.

Muscle loading and the storage of potential muscular and gravitational energy occur during the extended takeaway, the upswing, and the first part of the transition. The muscles must be stress-free before starting the swing to allow the joints to move freely and allow the main muscle groups to stretch to their maximum extent when they take the club to the top of the backswing.

THE EXTENDED TAKEAWAY

The arms and club are moved back together from the ball in a movement similar to a putting stroke.

The takeaway is initiated by rotating the thoracic spine and upper torso while constraining the motion of the pelvis, hips, and lower body. Consequently, at the start of the downswing, the motion sequence is automatically reversed, with the movement and rotation of the pelvis leading the upper body rotation.

The clubhead moves straight back for a short distance ahead of the hands. Consequently, when the clubhead is released on the forward swing, the hands lead the clubhead.

The takeaway ends when the upper body, arms, and club's combined weight moves into the right side. At this point, the player's right upper arm is held vertically, positioned close to the right chest, with the crook of the elbow facing outwards. The eyeline is parallel to the shoulders, oriented slightly to the inside of the target line.

By moving the clubhead straight back from the ball for a short distance, the left wrist remains flexed and cupped slightly during the takeaway. It assumes the correct position to begin the upswing and allows the wrists to cock and uncock to their full extent.

The Extended Takeaway

The extended takeaway is rehearsed in the following image on the right with the flexing or cocking of the left wrist to lift the clubhead and straighten the left arm. The player may also wish to move the arms and club to and fro to rehearse the baseline stroke and align it with the target line.

Maintaining flex in the left wrist ensures that the straight left arm and club rotate together during the swing.

As the arms and club move back together on the takeaway, the shoulder joints and the large muscles of the body are engaged to lift the arms and club together on the upswing.

THE UPSWING

The player moves smoothly and seamlessly into the upswing from the end of the takeaway. The chin, pointing to a point on the ground slightly inside the target line and a little outside the pinkie of the right foot, remains motionless to guide the upswing.

The right elbow and shoulder joints coil, forming a right angle between the forearm and upper arm, moving the hands to their high point. The momentum of the arms and club, lifted vertically together, automatically cocks the wrists to their full extent to complete the backswing.

The Upswing

The coiling or hinging of the right elbow moves the right shoulder back and around to rotate the upper torso and pivot the hips. The left knee moves forwards and inwards, and the right knee remains flexed. The straight left arm is automatically drawn upwards across the chest as the right elbow moves back and inside. During the upswing, the body's major muscle groups stretch due to the torque created by the coiling of the powerful core muscles of the abdomen.

The hands' height at their high point will depend upon the player's anatomy and the motion of his takeaway; refer to the section on Swing Style later in this chapter.

With the left wrist cupped, the vertical upward movement of the arms and club on the upswing keeps the player's weight directly above his right hip joint. It helps maintain the right knee flex and provides a stable base for the swing. With a stable base to the swing, smoothly accelerating the uplift speed will help continue the clubhead's rearward and backward momentum into the transition to maximize clubhead lag and acceleration on the forward swing.

As the backswing continues to completion, the left arm and club unit pivots freely about the left shoulder joint due to its momentum.

THE TRANSITION

When the hands have reached their high point, as shown in the first image, the clubhead's momentum moves it back and down behind the player completing the backswing; see the second image.

The clubhead pivots around the hinge point on the club's handle, cocking the wrists fully and reducing the lag angle between the clubshaft and the left forearm.

As the clubhead moves back and lower, the major muscle groups are stretched further to their maximum extent.

The transition changes the direction of the swing from the backswing to the forward swing. When the player senses the clubhead's weight and momentum behind him (second image), the seamless transition from the backswing to the forward swing begins (third image).

The Transition

The opening of the left knee to pivot the left hip initiates the transition and the kinetic chain. The left hip pivot rotates the upper torso, shoulders, and head by a small amount. There is a very slight lateral movement of the hips to the left as more weight moves downwards and into the player's left side. As the player transfers his weight to his left side, the right upper arm automatically moves closer to the chest's right side.

THE START DOWN

Ben Hogan considered the 'start down' the most important part of the swing. He was right in that the motion places the player in the ideal position to compress the ball to its fullest extent on the clubface.

The swing moves seamlessly from the transition to the start down when the player's eyeline is parallel to the target line.

Like the takeaway, the start down begins with the rotation of the thoracic spine but in the reverse direction. The right shoulder and elbow joints uncoil as the spine rotates, moving the right upper arm close to the chest.

The Start Down

There is no conscious pulling down of the club with the hands and forearms. The hands and wrists remain relatively 'quiet'. The left wrist's set remains; there is no unhinging or uncocking of the left wrist.

The head rotates while otherwise remaining still, pointing the chin slightly ahead of the ball, guiding the club's automatic release into the follow-through. At this point, the vertical right upper arm mirrors its position at the end of the takeaway.

THE EXTENDED-RELEASE AND FOLLOW-THROUGH

A sense of the right upper arm moving into the right side triggers the start of the clubhead's release. The right elbow unhinges, and the right forearm drives forwards to point the club towards the target line at the end of the follow-through. With the flex retained in the left wrist, the drive or thrust of the right forearm rotates the angled straight left arm and club as one unit around the left shoulder joint. Due to the flexed left wrist, the angle is maintained between the straight left arm and the club throughout the clubhead release.

With the right forearm drive and left arm and club pivot from the left shoulder joint working in unison, the clubface is delivered square to the target line at the low point of the swing arc.

The Extended Release and Follow-Through

As the clubhead is released, the player's weight is more centered. The right foot rolls to its inside to ready the foot and the leg to provide leverage to help clear the left side as the clubhead is released into the follow-through. This move prevents the hands, arms, and club from crossing over the spine, the body's centerline, too early and helps keep the clubhead stable and properly directed on a shallow arc along the target line in the strike zone. The stance and hips are naturally pivoted open slightly during the setup to facilitate an unencumbered extended clubhead release.

The thrust exerted by the right forearm drive and the upward thrust of the legs help to maintain a wide swing arc, slowing down the rotation of the clubhead and allowing the time and space for the correct delivery of the clubface square to the target line at the swing's low point.

The clubhead is fully released into the follow-through when its Center of Mass lines up with the player's swing center, positioned behind the sternal notch, and the left arm and club are aligned. The yellow dot in the image on the right represents the player's swing center.

For a straight shot such as this, an efficient, properly executed, automatically extended clubhead release will deliver the clubface square to the target line for the impact duration.

The clubhead's release is the true downswing. It releases the potential energy stored during the upswing and transition, increasing the momentum of the clubhead through impact.

THE FINISH

At the end of the extended-release and follow-through, the swing's momentum carries the arms and club upwards, around the body, into a well-balanced finish. The thoracic spine and upper body rotate and accelerate to the finish as the arms fold. The player is standing fully upright with his weight centered over the balance point at the finish.

The Finish

The swing's overall shape will vary depending on the player's anatomy and shot type. Every player will have their unique swing style or fingerprint.

SWING STYLE

The player's unique swing style is a function of his physical attributes. An individual's swing style is easily recognizable by his hands' position and height at the top of the backswing.

Taller players with long arms will have higher hands than shorter players with short arms. A player with a restricted hip pivot on his takeaway will have lower hands than a player who doesn't.

Generally, players who have a very strong coiling action of the core muscles in the abdomen don't need a long arm swing and high hands.

Often you will see accomplished players with swing styles that you might consider to be quirky. Some several highly-skilled ball-strikers and shot-makers have their unique swing idiosyncrasies. Players such as Moe Norman and Jim Furyk come to mind. What they are all seeking to do, in their unique way, is to deliver an efficient and effective clubhead release with lag tension sustained in the clubshaft and the clubface maintained square to the clubhead's elliptical arc of travel in the strike zone.

It is a common misconception that the player's swing style is entirely responsible for the shot outcome. Furthermore, the belief that there are thousands of swing styles, so there must be thousands of ways to teach and learn the golf shot is misplaced. The golfer must learn the stroke for the shot, not the swing. Please refer to the later chapter on learning smarter for more on this.

THE SWING CENTER, HAND PATH, AND SWING PLANE

As already alluded to, in the modern swing, the hands and arms don't swing the club; the body swings the arms and the club together, maximizing clubhead speed and acceleration. Contrary to common belief, the hand path is merely an outward expression of the swing driven by the bigger muscles of the body. It is not manipulated in any way other than to keep the swing dynamically balanced.

In the following series of images, we see the hands travel in a smooth wide curved path around the player's swing center. The swing center moves back away from the ball to maintain balance in motion. It moves to the right initially over the right hip as the backswing starts, before moving higher and towards the player's left side, above the left hip, on the forward swing. The hand path is not circular because of the sequential coiling and uncoiling of the right elbow and right shoulder and the consequent change in the swing center's position.

The hands travel in an upward spiral motion in the forward swing, on an arc tilted back slightly, away from the target.

The Hand Path

The swing is planar only during the bottom half when the clubshaft lies on an imaginary, flat, tilted plane. The swing plane then corresponds to the stroke and the shaft plane. The swing plane should not be confused with the swing path, which denotes the direction of the clubhead path when viewed from above.

The base of the inclined shaft plane is known as the plane line. The angle of inclination of the shaft plane, otherwise known as the vertical swing plane angle, depends upon the player's anatomy, the club, and the shot selected.

The modern golf swing uses the same fundamental on-plane and on-target stroke on every shot. It focuses mainly on the player's management and control of the stroke and shaft plane to control the shot shape and trajectory, not the swing path.

The Stroke and Shaft Plane

OVERALL SWING SHAPE

An extended takeaway and clubhead release widens the arc of the swing, so it corresponds more to an ellipse than a circle. A correctly executed extended takeaway and release shallows the swing's base and stabilizes the clubhead, maintaining the clubface square to the target line longer in the strike zone.

It means that the scope for error at impact is much less than is the case for the traditional rotary swing, where good timing is crucial for the strike's precise delivery. The distance the clubface remains near to square to the target line through the impact zone can be extended by as much as a foot on either side of the swing's low point. Refer to the graphic in Chapter 5 demonstrating the extent of a square clubface obtained with the driver through the impact zone.

The Swing Shape

THE KINETIC CHAIN

To understand the mechanics and dynamics of the swing, we have to understand the engine that is driving the swing. We accumulate and store potential energy on the backswing that we can call upon to drive the forward swing and deliver the precision golf stroke. The high-performance engine we use for this purpose is the kinetic chain.

When the player transitions the swing from the backswing to the forward swing, potential energy is automatically converted into kinetic energy to power the forward swing and the stroke.

The term 'chain' is potentially misleading. It is a seamless, uninterrupted motion that begins from the ground up, initiated by the opening up of the left knee and hip.

As demonstrated in the swing sequence, the kinetic chain starts before the player has completed the backswing. It begins when he senses the weight and momentum of the clubhead moving behind him. Note the changing position of the left knee in the sequence of images. The motion of the club must have momentum, moving back and down behind the player, to initiate the kinetic chain.

Initiating the Kinetic Chain

As the backswing ends and the forward swing begins, the clubshaft bends as the motion of the clubhead lags behind the grip end of the club.

Creating Lag Tension in the Clubshaft

The tension created in the clubshaft and its resistance to the change in direction to the forward swing causes the powerful shoulder and back muscles to contract to allow the arms and club to move past the chest freely, accelerating the clubhead through the ball.

As the clubhead accelerates into impact, the tension created in the clubshaft is preserved to sustain the straight line of compression. The extended takeaway and the automated conical pendulum release in the modern swing are the keys to sustaining lag tension in the clubshaft until after impact.

THE AUTOMATED CONICAL PENDULUM RELEASE

As the modern swing is shorter and more compact than its predecessors, an angle has to be maintained between the straight left arm and the clubshaft for the swing's duration.

As the takeaway extends, with the left wrist flexed, a cone is formed by the angle between the club and the straight left arm and the clubhead leading the hands moving back.

The preserved angle between the straight left arm and club creates a conical pendulum centripetal clubhead release, automatically triggered at the end of the start down and requiring no manual intervention. With the flex retained in the left wrist, the angled straight left arm and club pivot as a unit around the left shoulder joint as the right elbow and forearm extend and drive forwards towards the target line.

The Conical Pendulum Release

The release mechanism will produce a high clubhead speed and a solid strike even with relatively low arm speeds.

The acute angle formed between the straight left arm and the club at impact can be measured to check the release's efficiency.

Ideally, the angle at impact should be greater than 20 degrees; it will be slightly less for the driver than for irons. See the images below.

The Conical Pendulum Release
6-Iron

To sustain an angle greater than 20 degrees at impact requires a centripetal force to counteract the outward centrifugal force trying to straighten the left arm and club unit. The player can look to this angle as a useful clubhead lag and acceleration indicator. The greater the angle, the more the ball is compressed.

The lesser-skilled player may not have the core strength to execute a conical pendulum centripetal release, but there is no reason why boys and girls learning the game should not be able to. The key is to set the left wrist flex when starting the takeaway and maintain it throughout the swing.

Any loss of shape in the conical release such that the angle shown is less than 15 degrees will require manual intervention to square the clubface with the hands and forearms, with an attendant loss of clubhead lag and acceleration.

The stressed clubshaft will trail behind the left arm until the tension is released at the point when the angled straight left arm and club are in line with each other in the follow-through. The sustained lag tension in the clubshaft at impact can be seen in the center image.

Sustained Lag Tension in the Clubshaft at Impact

THE ROLE OF THE HANDS IN THE MODERN GOLF SWING

As you might expect, the hands have important roles in the modern swing, particularly how the player holds and applies pressure to the club.

The hands perform two important functions. They grip and appropriately hold the club to fashion the desired shape and trajectory of the shot. Secondly, they engender the player's feel for the swing and the stroke. Specifically, they sense changes in the swing and club's motion and provide feedback to the subconscious mind to balance the swing dynamically. The hands, arms, and legs should be strong, as they automatically guide the powerful stroke delivery without any conscious intervention or manipulation.

The phrase 'Grip it and Rip It,' normally associated with a desire to energize the swing to maximize distance, is a rather unfortunate turn of phrase. It denotes a course of action that is an aversion to the skilled shot-maker.

Unless the ball is buried deep in the rough when the club's blade must cut through the grass to reach the ball, a very firm grip is not something the player needs. The hands and arms will naturally become more active on iron shots as the strike is delivered with firmness to maximize the compression of the ball on the clubface. The main body muscles remain engaged to deliver the stroke.

The hands must not 'energize' the swing, as by doing so, the player will reduce the width of the swing, lose the angle between the straight left arm and club, and acceleration and clubhead lag tension are lost. The power created in the forward swing is partly a function of the player's ability to create and sustain clubhead lag by pivoting the angled, straight left arm and club unit around the left shoulder joint, not by pivoting the club around the hinge point on its handle.

The hands sense the body's movement and take appropriate actions to maintain it in equilibrium during the swing by resisting or facilitating the club's motion.

A major fault in the setup and takeaway can derail the swing from the outset, as the sensory feedback to keep the swing in balance is blocked.

If tension is allowed to creep into the grip, the player no longer fully controls the swing or the stroke, and his ability to perform his art is likely to be significantly diminished. It is perhaps worth emphasizing that while the hands and arms are relatively 'quiet' on the backswing and must remain free of tension and be receptive to sensory feedback, this does not mean they are not active.

There is no conscious rolling of the wrists and forearms in the strike zone; the wrists naturally firm up to deliver the steeper strike with an iron club, less so with woods and long irons as they have a shallower clubhead release direction.

Important elements of a well-balanced and stable swing are rhythm and tempo. Rhythm and tempo have different meanings.

THE IMPORTANCE OF DYNAMIC BALANCE, RHYTHM, AND TEMPO

Essential elements of good ball striking and shot-making are a stable swing, good balance, rhythm, and an even tempo. All these attributes are features of the modern swing, which is governed by the coiling and uncoiling of the powerful core muscles of the abdomen, allowing the hips to take over to initiate the downswing.

Rhythm relates to the synchronization of body movements to allow the body and club to rotate together in unison at the same rate, accepting that the hands and the clubhead are rotating around the body at different speeds.

A solid, precision golf stroke requires a stable, dynamically balanced swing. Tempo relates to the speed and timing of the swing. Regardless of swing speed, an even and smooth tempo is needed to complete the backswing and start the forward swing to maintain dynamic balance.

The following sequence of images is an excellent example of a dynamically balanced swing. While the head rotates very slightly at the start of the backswing and downswing, it otherwise remains still. There is no excessive lateral movement of the hips or swaying.

The player will automatically adopt a stance width corresponding to the club's length and the swing arc's anticipated width. The hips pivot during the setup to maintain an evenly balanced weight distribution.

Dynamic Balance in Motion

Medium Trajectory Straight Shot

Maintaining dynamic balance is aided by holding the chin independently of the swing's motion. There is a very slight head rotation to the right on the takeaway and starting the downswing. The chin directs the swing onto the correct path to complete the backswing and the forward swing. The top of the head remains in position during the swing. This little adjustment of the chin position as the head rotates at the start of the takeaway and the forward swing is very important. It acts as a stabilizer and is perhaps the most important element in the stroke's performance. It starts the arms, club, and clubhead back on the right line and helps keep the body relaxed, facilitating the automatic delivery of a solid, precision strike. It also automatically limits how far the arms can move on the backswing.

To execute a solid strike to maximize the ball speed and shot distance, the player will want to maximize the clubhead's speed and acceleration, consistent with keeping the swing balanced. In the modern swing, maximum clubhead speed and acceleration are the product of an efficient, automatic clubhead release, which occurs in the bottom half of the swing.

It is not achieved by 'energizing' the hands at the start of the forward swing. Striving to increase the clubhead's speed should not be done at the expense of upsetting the swing's dynamic balance.

The subconscious mind must be creative, open, and receptive to feedback; visualization and imagery have essential roles.

THE IMPORTANCE OF SENSORY AWARENESS AND FEEDBACK

The world's top ball-strikers and shot-makers are not overly concerned with technique or what the swing or club is doing. They are adept at 'getting out of their way' using visualization.

They instinctively understand the importance of enhanced sensory feedback and the role and power of the subconscious mind, the mind's eye. Their efforts are exclusively directed towards 'seeing and feeling' the shot. An important key to successful ball-striking and shot-making is to heighten the senses.

Do you think you can consciously deliver a clubhead traveling at over 100 mph to a point on the ball the size of a pinhead? Of course not; it is an absurd proposition.

The player needs to realize that the golf stroke's conscious direction of any kind will be a hindrance rather than a help. You might say that your subconscious mind controls your stroke delivery. Enhanced sensory awareness and feedback are essential for the player to perform successfully at a high level. Three senses, touch, sight, and hearing, must be fully and actively engaged. Recruiting all three senses during play and practice will aid muscle memory. It will enhance the player's 'feel' for a solid golf stroke, strike, and successful shot outcome.

Let's consider what is meant by this. You have a clear visual image of the ball flight you require, where you want the ball to land and finish. You establish an intermediate target on the ground ahead of the ball. You feel a connection between your body, arms, and the club as you move them back away from the ball to start your takeaway.

By relying on sensory input and feedback, you delegate control of the golf shot to the senses. Well done! You have just increased your shot reliability and accuracy by a significant margin and increased your shot distance.

Master ball-strikers and shot-makers possess an innate understanding of the stroke and the need to sustain the ball's compression. It does not mean that they necessarily fully understand the actual dynamics of the strike itself. What they do possess, though, is an exquisite sense of 'feel', balance, direction, timing, and precision that allows them to hit good shots consistently. The sense of 'feel' for the golf stroke and how the body moves must be acquired through repeated practice and playing the game. One of golf's greatest ball-strikers, Lee Trevino, offered his view: *"There is no such thing as natural touch. Touch is something you create by hitting millions of golf balls."* Golf Digest Feb 2013.

The use of visualization, imagery, and motor imagery also has a vital role. The player must use the mind's eye to 'see and feel' the shot. There are several examples of visualization the player can use. Perhaps the most important one is to visualize the intended ball flight. It is not enough to stand on the tee with the intent to hit the shot as far as possible. The player must visualize the intended height and shape of the shot and take note of the point on the ground where he wants the ball to land and finish. He must register any obstruction or hazard that might interfere with the shot and, if necessary, start again to avoid it.

Visualizing the target line etched on the ground stretching out ahead of and behind the ball is another example of how the player uses imagery to facilitate the shot.

Motor imagery is another important tool; the player mentally rehearses the action without physical movement.

Before starting the takeaway, the player should have a mental picture of the clubhead traveling directly back from the ball on the takeaway, and straight towards it and straight through it into the follow-through.

Such images provide the player with an external focus and prevent him from becoming preoccupied with his body positions, club alignments, and swing mechanics. They are essential components of skill learning and development.

Don't let yourself become self-absorbed during your round; open up and feel alive to what is happening around you. Stand and walk tall and open up the vista in front of you. Do not be tempted to rush and increase your tempo unnecessarily when under stress; doing so will narrow your field of vision and awareness and turn your perception in on yourself. Instead, keep your natural tempo and cadence even and controlled, and breathe normally.

The player feels the heft of the club and arms to connect them. A club that is too light will not provide this important sensory feedback. Subsequently, the player relies on sensory feedback or 'feel' from the hands and feet to maintain the relationship. Sensory feedback is easier if the player is alert, his muscles and joints are at ease in their movements, and there is no trace of stress or tension. Once the player has decided on the shot, his subconscious mind must remain open and be receptive to sensory feedback and new experiences.

Preparation for the task ahead is crucially important. Eating a big meal immediately before starting a round of golf is a temptation, as the player wants to store calories and build energy. Of course, energy diverted to the digestion of a big meal means less energy is available for powering the muscles and joints. A heavy meal also slows down the circulation, drawing blood and oxygen from the brain where it is needed most, leading to a loss of focus and concentration.

Tiredness is a major factor in poor performance on the golf course. When the player is tired, he loses focus, his senses are impaired, and the conscious mind takes over. It is important to have a thorough knowledge and understanding of how the stroke is configured for the intended shot and to devote extra attention to it during the setup when tired.

MENTAL FORTITUDE AND MINDSET

If the player wishes to compete at a high level, he must believe in and have confidence in his ability. Having the correct mindset will allow him to perform his art and develop his skills. His mindset must be on an efficient strike delivery and release. He must fully trust his swing to deliver it as required.

The skilled ball-striker and shot-maker who is fully prepared has supreme confidence in his ability to perform well. He is not intimidated by the golf course; he perceives it as a challenge to overcome rather than a difficulty to be faced.

He looks upon the entirety of the golf course as his artist's studio, where he practices his art, performs to his best, and produces his greatest achievements. He is not fazed by any shot, no matter how challenging

Skilled ball-strikers achieve success because they naturally acquire the blueprint for effective ball-striking and shot-making. They intentionally trust their ball-striking and shot-making abilities and make room for the subconscious mind to perform as it should.

Things go wrong when they lose that trust and attempt to deviate from their natural swing style. They will often lose their natural aptitude and ability and have great difficulty rediscovering what they have lost. Their self-belief and confidence will also be affected.

CONCLUSION

The modern swing and golf stroke, described fully in this chapter, offers versatility in shot-making, spin control, and increased shot distance. It is an automatic and reflexive response to the player's setup and takeaway.

The player can focus on learning and rehearsing the stroke for his intended shot rather than tinkering with his swing or changing it.

The next chapter explores how shot-making has evolved during the last hundred years or so, providing new insights into the golf shot.

CHAPTER 8: A SHORT HISTORY OF SHOT-MAKING

The chapter looks at how great golfers of the past, from Vardon to Hogan, controlled the golf shot and how The Shot-Maker's Code helps us understand their masterful ball-striking, shot-shaping, and spin control efforts.

Also, a brief look at scientific research on the spinning golf ball done in the late 19th Century by Professor Peter Guthrie Tait, inspired by his son Freddie, two-time Amateur Champion, and how it was relevant to The Shot-Maker's Code.

CHAPTER 8

A SHORT HISTORY OF SHOT-MAKING

With our recently discovered insights into stroke and strike dynamics, I decided to investigate the history of shot-making to see if I could find any clues to its development. Specifically, I wanted to research and observe the style of play of the master ball-strikers and shot-makers of an earlier era, when the game was fast gaining popularity on both sides of the Atlantic. What I found opened my eyes and gave me a fresh perspective on how the game was played. It also validated our findings and conclusions on shot-making, spin generation and control.

However, before I look more closely at the old masters and how they played, I must first consider what science was telling us about the golf shot at the time. Here we inevitably arrive at a man who, probably more than any other, was responsible for shining a light on the inner workings of the golf stroke and revealing the mysteries of the collision between the clubhead and the ball. That man was the eminent Scottish physicist and philosopher Peter Guthrie Tait (1831-1901).

THE LEGACIES OF PROFESSOR PETER GUTHRIE TATE AND HIS SON FREDDIE

His son, Freddy, inspired the learned professor's interest in the golf shot. Frederick Guthrie Tait (1870-1900), the youngest of three sons, was one of the world's top amateur golfers. He won the Amateur Championship on two occasions, in 1896 and 1898, and is credited with 28 tournament victories.

Sadly, Freddie was a casualty of the Boer War, losing his life in 1900 at the peak of his golfing prowess.

The professor was devastated by his son's death and died a few months later in the following year.

Through his regular contributions to popular sports journals and magazines of the day, the professor brought a wealth of knowledge to golfing enthusiasts.

As the learned professor sought to explain the science behind his son's long drives, he identified two sources of errant shot-making, recognizing the compounding effect of one on the other and the ability of one distinct stroke fault to cancel out the other. He described two very different stroke dynamics and spin modes that opposed or complemented each other.

Discounting the mishit and damaging gear effect, the idea of two different spin modes complementing or opposing each other piqued my interest, given their relevance to the precision, dynamic golf stroke, the core subject of this book.

The two stroke faults identified by the professor were considered, at the time, to be avoided at all costs. They were:

1. The hook or the slice due to a divergent clubface angle and club path
2. The hook or the slice, due to heeling or toeing, as a result of a divergent clubface and clubshaft orientation

We must bear in mind that for centuries, up until the mid-19th century, the Featherie ball was used. The ball was not receptive to changes in spin to curve the shot in a controlled way; hence there was only one acceptable shot, a straight one. Any curved golf shot was frowned upon and considered the preserve of the 'hacker'.

It was not until the invention of the hammer-hardened and machine-marked gutta-percha ball in the mid-19th century that players could learn how to control the ball's spin and intentionally shape the shot.

  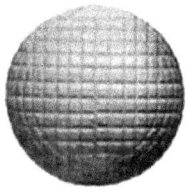

| Old Leather Ball | Hand-hammered Gutty | Machine-marked Gutty |

Source: Fifty Years of Golf, by Horace G. Hutchinson, London, 1919

In an article written for the Badminton Magazine in March 1896, the professor explained that the sliced and the heeled ball produced the same damaging left-to-right curve on the shot, but each had distinct spin characteristics. He explained that while the sliced ball would start its flight a little left of the intended shot direction before curving to its right, the heeled ball started its disastrous journey to the right of the intended direction and stayed right.

He cautioned his readers that the terms heeling and toeing were not to be taken literally, for heeling may be produced by the toe of the club and toeing by the heel. The observation has relevance to our findings. Indeed, we can construe from those wise words that heeling or toeing may be produced with a perfectly centered strike of the clubface to control the shot shape. If we can shape the shot in this manner, it follows that a heeling or toeing operation may also be applied with the vertical plane of the clubface to control the shot's trajectory and distance, whether the shot is shaped or not. Once we start to ponder the implications of the toeing and heeling operations identified by the professor, then the shadowy secrets of the stroke and strike are revealed to us.

Influenced greatly by his work and aided by the improvements in golf ball and club technology, the era of shot-making and spin control in golf had begun.

It is fascinating that the contributions made by the professor and his son are still the topic of conversation among R&A members even today. Freddie was the talk of St. Andrews for his record drive on the 13th hole of the Old Course made on his birthday on 11th January 1893. In no wind and on frozen ground, he recorded a distance of 341 yards with a carry of 250 yards. The following week his friend Andrew Lang wrote an article for the local newspaper recording the feat.

In the article, he cheekily inferred that Freddie's achievement went beyond what his father, the professor, considered physically possible according to the laws of physics.

To explain Freddie's prestigious carry and roll distance from the tee, we must examine his stroke pattern. The acclaimed golfing journalist J.L. Lowe wrote about this in Freddie's biography 'F.G Tait – A Record' published after his death in 1900. The author commented that Freddie had a style that others could not copy, no matter how much they tried. Fortunately for us, he provided a full description.

Freddie didn't swing the club back; he had a slow takeaway, drawing the club back directly from the ball with the powerful muscles of his back and shoulders. He also possessed a distinct follow-through extending the club forwards towards the target. The key to his long raking drives was his extended takeaway and follow-through. Deploying a strong right-hand grip and positioning his hands behind the ball, he set up for a high straight shot and used a forward push stroke to strike the ball forwards and upwards. (refer to the Glossary of Terms for the traditional meaning of push stroke) The result was a more penetrating shot trajectory and more roll and distance.

Experts that analyzed Freddie's stroke at the time named it the 'Rising Club Shot'. It is the same stroke that I have named the power runner in Chapter 5.

Of course, we are indebted to the learned professor and his son Freddie for their immense contributions to golf, especially for aiding our understanding of the golf shot.

HARRY VARDON

Harry Vardon (1870-1937), the most successful golfer of his era and a native of Jersey in the Channel Islands, possessed a unique swing style. He was the first true shot-maker and a master of many of the key elements of the modern swing and shot-making described in this book. Because the Gutty ball was more receptive to spin than its predecessor, the Featherie, Vardon adopted an overlapping grip to bring the hands closer together as a unit. He also changed from the wide, sweeping St. Andrew's swing style, adopting a shorter and more upright swing with an extended takeaway to provide greater utility for intentional shot-shaping. His right-hand grip naturally changed in the root of his fingers when he changed the forward or rearward tilt of the clubshaft to shape the shot or hit low or high trajectories.

Aided by the Gutty, the three members of the Great Triumvirate, Messrs. Vardon, Taylor, and Braid, teamed up to become some of the most notable shot-making and spin masters in the history of the game. How do we know this? Quite simply because it was explained to us in their books written at the start of the 20th century and still preserved for us today.

The American player Wild Bill Mehlhorn, considered by Ben Hogan to be the best player of his generation from tee to green, once said of Harry Vardon, whom he partnered on several occasions, *"He hardly ever misses a fairway."* He explained that was not an option when knee-high rough bordered the narrow fairway.

Images from the book, The Complete Golfer, by Harry Vardon, 1905
The Driver and Brassy, showing the stance and at the top of the swing.

By utilizing a takeaway and a stable, dynamically balanced swing oriented parallel to his target line painted as a white line in the images, he intentionally shaped the shot both ways, much to the admiration of his fellow tournament professionals.

He was also an acknowledged exponent and pioneer of the push shot, which many of his fellow touring professionals tried to copy.

He acquired the push shot during extensive practice on the range and on the course during his first two years as a professional. It was designed and configured to convert a low shot into a powerful mid-trajectory shot and give the ball stopping power on landing. He performed the shot with his cleek, equivalent to a long iron of today, although he could perform it with any club from any decent lie, including fairway bunkers.

His fellow touring professional Scotsman James Braid (1870-1950) was acknowledged by Mr. Vardon as the master of the push shot with the driver from the tee.

Later in his career, Vardon had to forsake his favored push shot, as the new ball, the American rubber-cored and wound Haskell ball known as the 'Bounding Billie', found its way across the Atlantic, much to the dismay of Vardon and others. The new ball would travel much farther than the Gutty, but it was not as receptive to spin control. It would also benefit a mishit with increased distance and bring more greenside bunkers into play. The observations intensely annoyed Vardon, who lamented that the Haskell ball cost him at least four strokes per round in tournament play.

Duncan. Taylor. Braid. Vardon.
Gutty v. Rubber Core
Source: Fifty Years of Golf, by Horace G. Hutchinson, London, 1919.

On the 2nd of April 1914, at Sandy Lodge Golf club in Hertfordshire, Vardon and Duncan played Braid and Taylor to test the distance of the Haskell rubber-cored ball. One couple used the Gutty and the other the Haskell in the morning, then changed them in the afternoon. Braid averaged about 25 yards less with the Gutty than with the Haskell.

The new ball was great for longer distances, but it wasn't easy to control. Unintentional big hooks and lost balls became a bane for many touring professionals when thick, knee-high rough often lined the fairways. To control the ball flight, Vardon dispensed with his extended takeaway and instead relied on his 'flat slice' from the tee, as did the vast majority of tour players on both sides of the Atlantic who copied him. The club was swung back inside the target line and 'looped' on the downswing to deliver the clubhead down the target line in the strike zone.

Although very different in terms of the shot execution, the ball flight resulting from the 'flat slice' is the equivalent of today's power fade. Vardon's shot-making prowess provided clear evidence of his ability to control spin effectively when the ball suited his skills.

The Englishman John H Taylor (1871-1963) was the acknowledged wizard of the short game. His skills were greatly admired by the British golfing public and by American tour players. Taylor pioneered the short, laid-back cut stroke played with the wedge from 80 yards or closer to the green. Golfing journalists of the era recounted how he would shoot directly for the pin and was able to stop the ball quickly.

BOBBY JONES

The next master shot-maker was the great American amateur golfer Bobby Jones (1902-1971). In his early career, Jones experimented and imitated the strokes of the best players who had preceded him, including Vardon. Much to the amusement of his Scottish teacher Stewart Maiden, Jones as a teenager, found that no matter how hard he tried, he couldn't emulate Vardon's push shot. The main reason for this is that Jones had more of a sweeping rotary motion to his swing, whereas Vardon's swing incorporated a takeaway and was more upright. Another reason is the different spin characteristics of the rubber-cored and wound Haskell ball compared to the Vardon Flyer, made of machine-molded rubber sap with a hardened cover.

Bobby Jones
Source: George Grantham Bain Collection (Library of Congress)

Jones went one better than his illustrious predecessor Vardon; he redesigned and streamlined his driver head to help him recreate the push shot and flight the ball lower to obtain more distance on his drives. This new driver shot was so reliable and successful; he went on to win 13 majors with it in just seven years.

Jones is the only player ever to complete the earlier form of the grand slam, four major victories in the same calendar year, in 1930. He perhaps pioneered what today is acknowledged to be the most dependable shot from the tee with the driver, the power runner.

We have a lot we can learn from the insights of Mr. Jones from the comments he made in his book, Golf is My Game, first published in 1959. His clear focus was always on striking the ball, not the swing.

"Golf is played by striking the ball with the head of the club. The objective of the player is not to swing the club in a specified manner, not to execute a series of complicated movements in a prescribed sequence, not to look pretty while he is

doing it, but primarily and essentially to strike the ball with the head of the club so that the ball will perform according to his wishes."

He added: *"I think the average golfer would present a more natural appearance if he should put his mind upon striking the ball rather than upon swinging the club."* He continued: *"Let the player always decide first upon the result he wants to produce; second, upon the precise manner in which he desires to strike the ball; and then let him place himself before the ball in such a position that he knows he will be able to deliver the blow in this manner."*

He likened the golf stroke to strokes in billiards and tennis: *"A person can no more play golf without a thorough knowledge of spin-inducing and spin decaying contacts than he could play billiards without an appreciation of the capabilities of follow and draw and a general idea of how a spinning ball will come off the cushions, or play tennis without knowing how his chops and twists are going to act."*

BEN HOGAN

Next on the scene was the modern-era maestro, the diminutive American Ben Hogan (1912-1997). Like his illustrious predecessor Harry Vardon, Hogan developed his swing, starting with the strike and building his swing from the ground up. After more than ten years of hard graft, trial and error on the practice tee, he acquired the most efficient and precise golf stroke ever witnessed before or since. His spin and distance control was unmatched and remains so even today.

The fear of the big hook led him to adjust his grip and takeaway. Aided by Vardon's push stroke, he finally mastered his famous power fade in the late 1940s and would become the world's most admired ball-striker and shot-maker.

The most impressive part of his new game was his control of trajectory, spin, and distance with his mid-iron clubs. It was entirely intuitive, based on his solid precision strike and the exquisite 'touch and feel' he had for the shot.

CONCLUSION

In this chapter, I have shared what I found about the shot-making skills of the old masters and their ability to use the stroke to control spin and produce long and very accurate shots.

Not surprising, then, the players of that era were masters of spin. Today with players striving to obtain more distance from the tee, the skill to control spin is alien to many. Without a doubt, they would all benefit from acquiring it. For example, if they knew how to compress the ball more to minimize spin with a driver, they could get an extra ten yards on the shot due to roll, if not more.

It was a great pleasure reading up on the old masters. I found it instructive that during the period I researched, over a hundred years ago, the players and the pundits alike spoke of the golf stroke, not the swing. Indeed, Bobby Jones famously remarked that he had no idea what the swing was; his focus was on correctly striking the ball. Due to the efficiency of his stroke and strike, his swing was natural and elegant and admired by his fellow players and fans worldwide.

CHAPTER 9: MR. HOGAN'S SECRET REVEALED

Mr. Hogan's search for perfection led him to pioneer the modern swing and stroke. The chapter explains how he overcame the dreaded hook with his trademark power fade shot.

While he encouraged the media to believe that his power fade was his secret weapon, he declined to reveal to them what was really behind his successes in the late 1940s other than to say he corrected a fault.

Based on the detail of his media interviews, the chapter reveals the secret he used with great success for the remainder of his playing career.

CHAPTER 9

MR. HOGAN'S SECRET REVEALED

To a large extent, the contents of this book reflect the legacy of Ben Hogan and the invaluable insights he bequeathed to us. We owe him a huge debt of gratitude. It is only fitting then that I should explore the secrets of his success.

Thousands of people have speculated upon Mr. Hogan's secret, and possibly dozens of books have been written on the subject, and the speculation has grown to mythical proportions. He shared various snippets of information with his friends and caddies but, by and large, kept the media guessing.

The secret of his success as a player was undoubtedly about Ben Hogan, the man, and his perseverance, hard work, and dedication, as it was about the specific adjustments to his swing. After ten years of diligent practice and hard work on the golf range and helped by advances in ball technology, Mr. Hogan created a perfectly balanced swing and a powerful precision golf stroke. It enabled him to control the spin rate, spin axis, and resultant ball flight and shot distance with amazing consistency and accuracy. A feat that has remained elusive to even the world's best golfers today.

Mr. Hogan was famed for 'digging it out of the dirt'. He spent thousands of hours practicing hitting better and more reliable shots. His swing mechanics and dynamics adapted naturally as his ball-striking and shot-making improved.

During the 1940s, Mr. Hogan finished as the leading money winner on the PGA Tour five times. In January 1947, he was flying high when his trusted driver broke, and he couldn't find a suitable replacement. Having had thirteen wins in the previous year, he soon found himself eclipsed by players such as Jimmy Demaret and the newcomer to the tour, South African Bobby Locke.

A low hook plagued him from the tee during the year. He was so discouraged that he decided to leave the tour in early September and return home to Fort Worth. During his two-week stay at home, he managed to find a permanent fix by embedding what was to become his trademark shot from the tee, a powerful mid-trajectory fade. He was so encouraged by his newfound shot that he couldn't wait to get up in the morning to practice, spending six to eight hours on the practice range for several days.

His practice was productive. He won his next tournament, the World Championship of Golf in Chicago, by three shots. Just over a month later, in early November 1947, when captaining the U.S Ryder Cup team, he confided in Joe Novak, the PGA Secretary, that he had finally learned how to play golf by mastering the power fade.

1948 went on to be his second-best year on tour, winning ten tournaments during the year, including the U.S. Open at Riviera Country Club. It was surpassed only by his thirteen wins in 1946. Despite being seriously injured in a vehicle accident in 1949, Mr. Hogan achieved many more successes in the 1950s.

Journalists, impressed by his performances, were keen to discover his secret.

In his famous article for Life Magazine in August 1955, he explained the swing adjustments he had made earlier in 1946. Surprisingly he was a year out; the historical record shows that he made the changes in September 1947.

He told a story about finding a solution when lying awake in bed at his home. He identified two adjustments that still allowed for the normal pronation of the left wrist and the slight opening of the clubface on the takeaway.

1. *A left-hand grip adjustment*
   He moved his left hand a fraction of an inch to the left on the club, positioning his left thumb almost directly on top of the clubshaft.
2. *Gradual cupping and cocking of the left wrist later in the backswing*
   For a fade, after completing the takeaway, he consciously and gradually rolled in the left wrist and forearm, producing a cupped left wrist at the top of the swing. For a draw, he made no conscious effort to roll the wrist and forearm inwards on the upswing.

THE SECRET MR. HOGAN DIDN'T REVEAL – HIS EXTENDED BASELINE STROKE

In 1948 Mr. Hogan gave a hint to the press as to why he was playing better than ever. In June 1948, after winning the U.S. Open at the Riviera Country Club in Los Angeles with a record score, a journalist asked him why he was playing better golf during the last two years than previously. Mr. Hogan explained, *"I used to hit a ball that would hook or fade and drop too quickly. Now I can keep the ball up there longer, and it, therefore, stays true to the line and usually comes to rest just about where I want it."*

When asked what he did to achieve that, his reply was interesting in what it did not reveal. *"That",* he said, *"Is a secret. Nobody's going to get that. All I can say is that I have corrected a fault."*

His preferred weak right-hand grip, adopted several years earlier in 1939 on the advice of his friend and mentor Henry Picard, was likely the main reason he couldn't keep the ball airborne for longer. In September 1947, he had solved his problem with the help of an extended, on-target baseline stroke, converting low as well as high shots into powerful mid-trajectory shots that would hold their line for longer. Perhaps without knowing it, Mr. Hogan had adopted the same push stroke pioneered by Harry Vardon over a half-century earlier. The two modern equivalents of the push stroke, the power spinner and the power runner, are described in Chapter 5: Advanced Shot-Making.

In his first book, Power Golf, written in 1947 and published in 1948, Mr. Hogan provided a clue as to the evolution of his swing. He described how he would vary his swing path and grip strength to draw or fade the shot. That was to change; before the end of 1947, he had adopted his one swing concept allowing him to create a powerful mid-trajectory fade or draw without changing his swing path or intentionally opening or closing the clubface.

In his second book, The Modern Fundamentals of Golf, published in 1957, he explained his stroke, which was basically describing the extended baseline stroke. Hogan commented, *"In its general character, the correct motion of the right arm and hand in the impact area resembles the motion an infielder makes when he throws half sidearm, half underhand to first after fielding a ground ball. As the right arm swings forward, the right elbow is very close to the right hip and 'leads' the arm – it is the part of the arm nearest target."*

Ben Hogan's 'Extended Baseline Stroke'
Source: The Modern Fundamentals of Golf, by Ben Hogan. London, 1957

The extended baseline stroke is a forward stroke oriented towards the target for every shot regardless of the desired shot shape. It is self-evident that the stroke is not consistent with a change in swing path from in-to-out or out-to-in for shot-shaping, with the associated closing or opening of the clubface.

Mr. Hogan said as much in his book. He explained, *"the golfer has to learn only one swing. HE USES THE SAME FUNDAMENTAL SWING FOR EVERY SHOT HE PLAYS. Once the average golfer is properly started on the correct method of hitting the golf ball, he will gradually find that he is able to hit the ball high, low, draw it, fade it, play sand shots, recoveries, half shots - ALL THIS WITHOUT CHANGING HIS SWING. The swing itself is what gives you this feel for managing this full variety of shots."*

With a solid, centered, precision strike, aided by sustained lag tension in the clubhaft, the impact interface between the clubface and the ball remained stable, facilitating a very efficient energy transfer.

By maximizing compression, Mr. Hogan used the club as a multi-functional tool to independently change the ball's launch angle and launch direction.

CONCLUSION

In short, the true secret of Mr. Hogan's remarkable success was his mental strength, his target focus, and the precision and dynamism of his strike, facilitated by the extended baseline stroke he used for every shot. It was the key to controlling the ball flight with a high degree of accuracy and consistency. His exquisitely balanced and stable swing enhanced his exemplary ball-striking and shot-making skills.

Mr. Hogan applied himself to mastering the golf shot during more than ten years of intense and focused practice on the range and the course, taking him to levels of performance that were unheard of at the time. The golfing world owes him a huge debt of gratitude for his legacy, which has benefited today's great ball-strikers and shot-makers and has informed how many of us play the game.

His real achievement in mastering the golf shot was that he systematically eliminated unnecessary movement in his swing, reducing the complexity of the strike. By simplifying the swing and strike, he was able to focus his attention more on his intended target and call upon his feel and senses to control the shot. To better understand how he achieved this, we only have to consider Mr. Hogan's extended baseline stroke in the context of The Shot-Maker's Code Blueprint in Chapter 3.

In 1982, Mr. Hogan became a mentor of Kris Tschetter, a fellow member of the Shady Oaks Country Club in Fort Worth, Texas. At the time, she played as a freshman at Texas Christian University. Later she would go on to win on the LPGA Tour. Their close friendship was to endure for over ten years until his death in 1997. Perhaps more than any other living person, apart from his wife Valerie, Kris knew Mr. Hogan for what he was, a deeply caring man and a giant in the game of golf, and a true legend.

CHAPTER 10: LEARNING SMARTER

A fresh approach towards learning the golf shot by learning the stroke for the shot, not the swing.

A roadmap to smarter learning is offered with a progressively structured program for skill development.

CHAPTER 10

LEARNING SMARTER

This chapter aims to help guide the reader on a path of improvement based on learning the stroke, not the swing. It may also be of interest to golf teachers who wish to expand their knowledge of the golf shot.

Many golfers spend years tinkering with their swing, all to no avail. They often fail to realize the importance of the stroke to the golf shot and how it's formed.

The stroke-centered learning of the golf shot has three important fundamentals which guide the process:

1. The golf shot is mastered by learning the stroke, not the swing. The motion of the swing automatically responds to the intended stroke.
2. The foundation for learning the golf shot is the baseline precision golf stroke. It must be continuously reinforced with practice.
3. The shot shape and trajectory are determined not by how the player swings or manipulates the clubface but mainly by how he aims, holds and positions the club during the setup.

The chapter offers a new approach to learning the golf shot, recognizing our improved knowledge of stroke dynamics. We would all do well to follow the sage advice of English Master PGA professional and golf teacher Luther Blacklock whose mantra is *"Learn the shot; the swing's for free."*

Our novel approach to learning, which has been thoroughly tested and validated on the golf course, emphasizes sensory perception and feedback and the player's approach to configuring and executing the stroke rather than being overly attentive to the swing's motion. It has the potential to revolutionize how the game is taught and learned. The change, if made, will be productive. The results will speak for themselves.

As everyone is different, every player has a swing style and a way of playing the game, which is dictated by their nature, personality, and biomechanics. Learning the swing according to a predefined model risks changing the player's natural swing style. Hence, it is important to learn the stroke and configure it. The swing will take care of itself. A more natural 'stroke and ball' approach to ball-striking and shot-making based on intuition, touch, and feel is needed, compared to a more contrived and stilted 'body, club and swing' geometric focus, which forms the basis for much of golf instruction today.

The player's mindset is perhaps the most important part of learning the golf shot in a formal structured setting. The student must be keen to learn and dispel any negative thoughts about his abilities or performance. He must be open and receptive to new ideas and experiences, including using his senses wisely to acquire a 'feel' for the stroke and strike relevant to a specific shot type.

REITERATIVE LEARNING

The scope of learning and teaching the golf shot must be clearly defined. It must have clear boundaries to be effective. The smart learning process for The Shot-Maker's Code is quite simple. The student must understand and embed the baseline precision golf stroke as the foundation for shot-making. It must be carefully calibrated to align with the target as part of the setup process.

The student golfer can learn a lot from the setup and takeaway process. Ultimately, the skilled shot-maker is not defined by what his swing looks like but by his setup and takeaway. A skilled shot-maker will display supreme confidence and flair when setting up for the shot.

The learning process is reiterative; as the player's skills in configuring and executing the stroke are practiced and improved, the player's setup and the takeaway process will also improve. As his setup process becomes more efficient, his stroke delivery and shot-making skills will benefit.

The learning process often fails because the golfer strays from the essential fundamentals that need only be learned, practiced, and assimilated to become intuitive and second nature. When that point is reached, the player is ready to use his imagination and creative skills to 'see and feel' the shot. The subconscious mind assimilates the baseline precision golf stroke, the foundation and determinant of all shots.

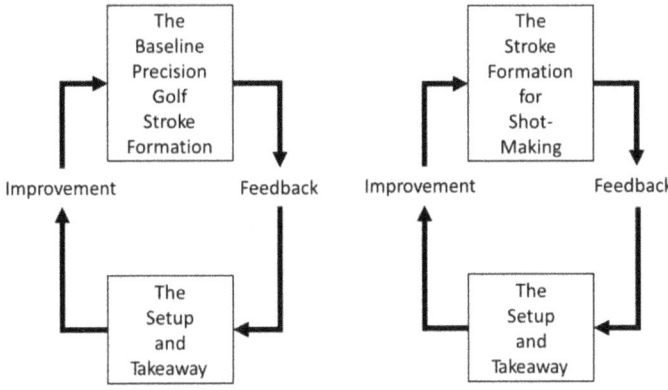

THE GRIP

As the hands are the only point of contact with the club, the positioning of the grip is crucially important.

If the player stands upright, tilts forward, and allows his arms to hang naturally, the wrists turn inwards slightly. The left hand is positioned on the club in the same attitude. The club is held mainly in the palm, with the handle resting in the crook of the forefinger and the thumb, positioned on the right side of the clubshaft.

The biomechanically correct left-hand grip position doesn't change.

In the right hand, the club is held in the root of the two middle fingers. By rotating the right wrist, the hand can be positioned more on top of the club (weaker) or more beneath it (stronger). The intelligent matching of the right-hand grip strength with the forward or rearward clubshaft tilt is the key to shot shaping or obtaining a straight shot on target.

The grip pressure must be relatively light, such that the muscles in the forearms and wrists remain free of tension.

ESTABLISHING A FEEL FOR THE GOLF STROKE

Having learned how to grip the club correctly, the student can engender a 'feel' for the stroke. The process starts with learning how to putt, starting with short putts and progressing to longer putts. The intention is to get the student used to stroking the putter and arms together as one unit with the shoulders and back muscles rather than relying on the hands and arms alone. Once the student has developed a good putting stroke, the stroke is extended to short chip shots and longer chips and pitch shots while choosing a small target on the green to land the ball.

Once the student has a 'feel' for the stroke, he can extend the swing to produce half, three-quarter, and then full iron shots. He progresses onto fairway woods and the driver when he is comfortable with iron shots.

A feel for the stroke is obtained by rehearsing the motion of the clubhead in the strike zone, one or two feet on either side of the low point of the swing arc.

PURPOSEFUL PRACTICE

Mastery of the great variety of strokes requires practice. If the player wishes to derive maximum benefit from practice, it must be done with a clear purpose. Maximum benefit is derived from regularly practicing the setup and takeaway process and calibrating the baseline stroke to the intended target with the help of alignment sticks and tee-pegs.

A useful approach to practice is replicating different playing situations with various strokes. For example, when practicing shot-shaping, use imagery and imagination, such as hitting a high draw over an imaginary bunker to a pin positioned on the left of an imaginary green. Practice adding or removing spin on short approach shots, e.g., a low spinning fade to a back pin position or a short high spinning punch shot to stop the ball quickly close to a pin positioned on the front of the green. It is also good to practice different shots to combat or harness the wind, even with no wind.

Hitting a few shots with a weighted iron can help to ingrain the feel for the correct move away from the ball.

Players should not be tempted to beat balls in quick succession, one after the other, with no real objective in mind. The time allotted for a practice session should be limited.

After a hundred shots, most players will start to tire and lose focus, so it is vitally important to know when to stop. When tired, the player will tend to grip the club harder, creating tension in the arm muscles. The wrists and forearms must remain relaxed and 'quiet'.

One of the most important parts of the scoring game, and one area that typically requires the most practice, is the short game and putting.

FAULT FIXING

Stroke faults are generally traced to an unstable stance and swing, poorly fitted clubs, or the setup and takeaway process. Rather than looking for a Band-Aid to fix a stroke fault or perceived swing fault, the player has only to return to the stroke fundamentals and recalibrate the baseline golf stroke. The process is comparable to retuning a car's engine.

RECALIBRATING THE BASELINE STROKE

A medium trajectory straight shot is used to recalibrate the baseline stroke, emphasizing a stable stance, good rhythm, and an even tempo. Ensuring the student has warmed up and removed any tension from the muscles, the process is as follows:

1. The Setup

    Tilting forwards from the hips, the player aims the clubface toward the intermediate target (marked by a tee peg) and positions and adjusts the grip and club to obtain the desired shot outcome. In this example, the player has neutral, matching left-hand and right-hand grips and no clubshaft tilt to obtain a medium trajectory straight shot. The Vs formed by the forefinger d thumb of each hand point towards the left ear when viewed from face-on.

2. The Extended Takeaway

    The player moves the clubhead straight back for a short distance, allowing the clubhead to lead the hands. The arms and club are moved or taken straight back together as a unit, not swung back. As the takeaway begins, the clubhead must not move to the inside or outside of the rearward extension of the target line. The main faults in the takeaway are swinging the club back with the hands and arms activating the wrist joints. The hands and wrists must remain relatively 'quiet' and free of tension.

3. The Follow-Through

The follow-through ends when the right arm has straightened shortly after impact before the wrists start to recoil. There is no conscious rolling of the right wrist or forearm.

Recalibrating the Baseline Precision Golf Stroke

When recalibrating the baseline stroke, common errors to look for are:
- A poorly fitting club
- Lack of target awareness and orientation
- Errors in the positioning of the clubface and clubshaft
- Errors in the positioning and adjustment of the grip
- Errors in the direction of the sightline relative to the ball
- Errors in the stance position and adjustment
- Tension in the muscles, gripping the club too tightly
- Incorrect tee height

PREVENTING THE BIG MISS

A player capable of hitting long drives has a considerable advantage over a player who is much shorter from the tee. The big hitter is looking to find the fairway, but it is not always a priority. A long drive finishing in the light rough can be more advantageous than finding the short grass with a shorter drive. The main objective then with the driver is to avoid shots that are likely to cost one or more dropped shots, e.g., a drive finding water, thick rough, or a deep bunker. There is little value in opting for a shorter club from the tee unless you find it difficult to control shots with the driver.

Most golfers find it much easier to control an iron shot from the fairway than the driver from the tee without really understanding why. Many people will attribute it to the higher swing speed, the length of the club, or differences in the clubhead's shape.

The common errors identified in the previous section can all contribute individually or collectively to a wayward shot with the driver, not least because they all make it much more difficult to produce a solid centered strike on the ball with the sweet spot of the clubface, located at or close to its center.

When the clubface is struck off-center with a deep-faced club such as the driver, the collision force deflects or twists the clubhead, changing the ball's launch angle and direction and its spin rate and spin axis, often by a significant margin.

The risk of a mishit is less when the body's setup and motion are stable and balanced, allowing the club and clubhead's unencumbered release into the follow-through.

Ideally, the driver must be properly fitted to suit the player's comfort, ability, and skill level. Clubfitters estimate that a club length that is too long causes 95% of the off-center ball impacts with the driver. The standard length of the driver clubshaft is 45-inches, and even longer ones are found on sale. Most players would benefit from the shorter 44.5-inch clubshaft commonly used by PGA Tour players. The length of the clubshaft is fitted to improve the impact location on the clubface using decals. Any length adjustment may require an adjustment in the swing weight to rebalance the club.

Several factors usually combine to create a big miss from the tee, including strong winds. The lack of awareness of cause and effect may instill a sense of fear in the player with the driver in hand. Because of fear, players tend to grip the club tighter and subconsciously steer or misdirect their swing to avoid a hazard on a particular side of the hole. For example, when there is out-of-bounds on the left side of the hole, fear of going left might cause the player to inadvertently open the clubface and slice the shot to the right. Alternatively, he might swing to the right and create a hook.

It is less likely that the player will succumb to fear if he has mastery of the setup and takeaway process and is confident in his shot-making skills.

The good news is that all of these common faults experienced by every level of player can be entirely avoided by returning to the basics and recalibrating the baseline golf stroke, having been correctly fitted for the driver.

CLUB FITTING AND BALL SELECTION

Mastering the skills of shot-making and spin control requires the correct equipment. A professional clubfitter must customize and fit the club to the player.

A ball is selected to suit the individual player's standard. There is no point in practicing shot-making or fixing faults with an inferior-quality club or ball. Ideally, the golf course, not the golf range, is the place to learn spin and distance control.

There is no need to worry about the ball's exact compression rating. A low compression-rated ball will help maximize the shot distance for those with a slow swing speed. A medium compression-rated ball is the standard ball for most golfers, both male and female, with average strength and swing speed.

Tests by manufacturers have shown that handicap players and skilled players alike might benefit and improve their performance by using a modern premium quality golf ball. Ball choice has a positive impact when the player sticks with a preferred brand and model. It's far better to get acclimated with a ball to how it feels and responds than to switch between different models or brands. The key reasoning is that the player acquires a feel of how the ball spins and how it responds to the strike.

JUNIOR GOLF

Young children need not be taught the golf shot. They are born mimics, and if they are exposed to watching good players, they will learn good habits by imitation.

When young boys and girls start to play the game as young teenagers, they are natural ball-strikers. Their shot-making skills improve as their clubhead speed increases, and they obtain a better 'feel' and an 'eye' for the shot. Because it is mechanically efficient, dynamic, and versatile for shot-making, young students should be encouraged to learn the modern golf stroke and experiment with controlling the ball flight to develop their shot-making skills.

Problems often arise when well-meaning teaching professionals make unnecessary changes to the young player's swing style and interfere with their natural ability.

Because they are supple and athletic, many youngsters have very high clubhead speeds and acceleration; this should be encouraged to maximize distance and create the strike and impact dynamics required for shot accuracy and reliability. Young players can initially expect wayward shots, but as hand-to-eye coordination, balance, and precision improve, this will be less problematic.

When possible, young players who demonstrate a natural aptitude for the game should be using good quality premium golf balls on the golf course. Any exercise to strengthen and flex the core muscles of the abdomen, such as a series of sit-ups, will also benefit the young golfer.

Perhaps the best advice to give to a young player is to enjoy the learning process. While the game can cause frustration at times, the rewards for playing well are more than worth the effort.

POTENTIAL IMPEDIMENTS TO LEARNING

Perhaps the main impediment to learning the golf shot is the continued reliance on methods that focus on swing and club geometry. Not enough attention is given to how the ball is struck and compressed on the clubface. Most of the methods taught to golfers are swing-centered, not stroke-centered. A swing-centered approach generally lacks appreciation or understanding of the golf stroke, its formation and delivery, and the important dynamic relationship between the clubhead and ball during impact.

In 1991, the PGA of America's Manual of Golf was published, explaining how the golf shot should be taught and learned. It drew from the accumulated experience of its Members over more than 70 years since its founding in 1916.

The model for teaching, documented in the manual, is the celebrated PGA of America Ball Flight Laws, showing how the golfer can control the shot distance and direction by varying the swing path and clubface orientation relative to the target and varying the angle of approach.

As a global standard for golf instruction, the manual is used as a reference by many thousands of golf teachers worldwide.

Based upon recent advances in golf impact science and considering the evolution of the modern swing, which is stroke-centered, not swing-centered, there are now opportunities to update the teaching philosophy and model recommended by the PGA of America.

Today the launch monitor has a major role in assisting the golfer's learning process and skill development.

They have become so popular that almost every tour player and golf teacher has access to one. A launch monitor is an excellent tool for tracking the ball flight and downrange results. However, as many teachers know, some caution is required when using swing and club metrics produced by launch monitors to inform the golf shot. Ideally, the student should not be exposed to swing and club data, as it potentially risks distracting him from where his true focus should be, configuring the golf stroke to control the ball flight.

CONCLUSION

The game has evolved with new technology and better equipment. The looping, sweeping swing of yesteryear was, at the time, the appropriate way to use the weight of the heavier club and gravity to power the motion of the swing. Today we have longer and lighter clubs, making it necessary for the player to engage the main muscle groups to power the swing.

A fresh, more natural, and straightforward approach to golf instruction is sorely needed, emphasizing the importance of a correctly configured and executed golf stroke and a natural, seamless setup and takeaway process.

The player must have the correct mindset to learn the stroke to obtain his desired ball flight and resist tinkering with, and changing, the motion of his swing.

For decades, golf has been taught and learned in a contrived way that often fails to recognize the player's innate abilities, intuition, and 'feel' for the golf shot, which is a sure way to suppress the player's flair and creativity.

As the great Bobby Jones remarked: *"Today, regretfully, more often than not, golf is not taught in the natural way it should be learned. It is taught more as a science or as a prescribed set of calisthenic exercises, whereas it is learned as a game"*.

Armed with an improved understanding of the blueprint for shot-making, the player can learn how to control the ball flight through experimentation and self-discovery.

Swing faults are more likely to be stroke faults; they are corrected not by tinkering with the swing over days, months, and years but by simply recalibrating the baseline stroke.

We can learn a lot from the old-school master ball-strikers and shot-makers who learned by imitation and ultimately developed their self-taught way of executing the golf stroke, relying upon exquisite touch and feel for the club and shot. Today, we tend to be constrained by what we perceive to be the way we should learn.

We can indeed learn a lot by heeding the golfing greats' advice to experiment, learn, and have trust in our unique abilities.

SUMMARY OF KEY INSIGHTS

Chapter 2: Understanding Impact Dynamics
- The spin imparted on the ball is a product of where on the ball it is struck, and the magnitude and direction of the force imparted at that point during the entire period of impact.
- The spin rate and the resultant ball flight are influenced by the conditions of impact, i.e., the rotation of the clubhead during impact and the magnitude and direction of the compressive force. This unlocks a deeper understanding of how spin is being generated by the club.
- Failure to grasp this means that whatever the golfer is trying to do with changes to swing direction, club path, and angle of attack, it will not be clear. Swinging and hoping for the best is not a real solution and is a poor foundation for building golf skills.
- Clubhead lag and sustained lag tension in the clubshaft are essential ingredients of impact geometry and dynamics. Clubhead lag is required for clubhead acceleration. A decelerating clubhead will produce a poor shot.
- The modern golf stroke utilizes lag tension in the clubshaft and impact geometry and dynamics to sustain the line of compression during the entire duration of impact.
- The stroke delivery is fully automated, requiring no conscious manual intervention.

Chapter 3: The Shot-Maker's Code Blueprint
- The Shot-Maker's Code Blueprint defines the constant and variable parameters that are applied to the golf stroke for shot-making.
- The blueprint is not a process, method, or technique. It represents the definitive design of the golf stroke to create any type of shot.

- Having acquired the blueprint, the golfer can configure the stroke during the setup to create any shape or trajectory of shot and control how the ball behaves when it lands.
- An on-target baseline precision golf stroke is established for every shot, regardless of its intended shape or trajectory. It incorporates four stroke constants. Two of the constants relate to how the club is held in the left hand and the aim of the clubface. The other two create a balanced setup and swing and extend the width of the swing arc, shallowing the base of the swing.
- Only three stroke variables are required for shot-making and distance control, relating to the right-hand grip strength, the clubshaft tilt, and the player's sightline. Each variable can be adjusted to any one of three positions and combined in various ways with the remaining two variables.
- The player's stance and ball position and the subsequent motion of the swing all adapt naturally and intuitively to the player's setup, takeaway, and strike delivery intent.
- The golf stroke is consciously formed to be subconsciously delivered.
- The swing is a reflexive, natural, and automatic response to his previously configured stroke and takeaway and the player's visualization of the intended ball flight and shot result.
- The shot-maker engages the body's main muscle groups to create and deliver the stroke. He does not direct the swing or manipulate the clubface with the hands or arms.

Chapter 4: Basic Shot-Making

- Basic shot-making addresses the control of the shot's direction, shape, and trajectory.
- The baseline golf stroke, anchored by the sightline and focal point, forms a solid foundation for every shot and unlocks the secrets of skilled shot-making with the precision and dynamism of the stroke.

- The stroke and strike delivery are rehearsed with the clubhead lift and waggle.
- When deploying the baseline golf stroke, control of the shot's direction, shape and trajectory is essentially about how the golfer holds and positions the club and aims the clubface during the setup to balance the club and achieve the desired shot outcome.
- It is a far simpler and more efficient approach than trying to swing the club in a prescribed manner by directing the swing path and manipulating the clubface. It altogether avoids the more complicated process of adjusting and aligning the stance, the shoulders, and the ball position during the setup.

Chapter 5: Advanced Shot-Making
- Specialty shots, incorporating the baseline precision golf stroke, are deployed to control the spin rate, shot trajectory and distance, and the behavior of the ball when it lands.
- Two variations of the power shot control the ball's spin rate and stopping power on the longer shot. The same principles apply to the short punch shot and the running pitch or chip shot. On shorter shots of 80 yards or less, the short, laid-back cut shot performs a similar role.
- Power shots and the short, laid-back cut shot change the ball's launch angle and spin rate in a controlled way, utilizing the strike's precision, dynamics, and efficiency.
- The hallmark of a good ball-striker and shot-maker is a player who can keep the spin rate and ball flight stable, optimizing the shot distance and judging how far to roll the ball when it lands.

Chapter 6: Taming the Wind
- Understanding the effects of the wind on the golf shot and knowing how to harness or combat it are essential skills for the shot-maker.

- If the option is open to him, the player should select a longer or shorter club to counteract a headwind or tailwind, respectively. Otherwise, to hold its line against a strong headwind, the shot must be launched lower and higher down a tailwind.
- A direct crosswind has only a marginal effect on the overall shot distance. However, it can push the shot offline a considerable distance.
- The target line and setup alignment are offset towards the wind to counter a strong crosswind. The amount of offset will vary depending on the wind speed and direction, the club selected, and the shot trajectory. Typically, between one and one and a half yards offset will be needed for each mph of direct crosswind speed to return the shot towards the actual target. The yardage offset will be less for a wind quartering from ahead or behind.
- On short approach shots, the player increases the spin rate with the wind behind to avoid the ball dipping down steeply and falling short. The spin rate is reduced into a headwind to prevent the shot from ballooning out of control.
- Long and short power shots are ideal shots to use to control the spin rate when it's windy. They are noted for their penetrating mid-trajectory ball flight.

Chapter 7: The Modern Golf Swing

- The modern golf swing is very different from the traditional rotary swing, not least because it generates more power, with leverage provided on the downswing by the powerful muscles of the legs and glutes.
- Assisted by an extended takeaway, the modern swing is stroke-centered, not swing-centered. The stroke required for the desired shot is configured beforehand during the setup to automate the swing.
- The swing must not be interfered with. It is a natural, automatic, reflexive response to the setup and takeaway.

- The foundation of the modern swing is the baseline precision golf stroke applied for all shots. Using the club as a multi-functional tool, shots are worked around the baseline stroke to change their shape or trajectory. The club does the work, not the swing.
- As the extended takeaway has moved weight into the player's right side, the right arm and shoulder control the arms' and club's vertical up and down motion and the body's rotation. The left arm and shoulder have a largely passive and reactive role.
- As the swing is shorter, wider, and has less depth than the traditional rotary swing, a conical pendulum release is needed to sustain lag tension in the clubshaft and sustain the line of compression of the ball on the clubface.
- The angled straight left arm and club unit, formed during the setup and maintained during the takeaway and throughout the swing to pivot about the left shoulder joint, is the foundation of the conical pendulum release.
- The modern swing requires a solid, stable base and an even tempo when transitioning from the backswing to the downswing in order to maintain dynamic balance in motion.
- The modern swing relies on high sensory awareness and feedback. The player must remain alert and open to sensory feedback to allow the subconscious mind to process feedback efficiently. He establishes a feel for the club and the shot.
- The modern golf swing and stroke offer versatility in shot-making, spin control, and increased shot distance.

Chapter 8: A Short History of Shot-Making
- The best players of the late 19th and early 20th Century were masters of spin control and pioneers of shot-making made possible by advances in golf ball design and manufacturing.
- Three players, in particular, stand out among their peers as pioneers of the modern game. Messrs Vardon, Jones, and Hogan. Other players such as Snead, Nicklaus, Palmer, Player, and latterly Woods achieved great success in recent decades, helped by further advances in equipment design and performance as well as with their own superior athletic prowess and performance.
- The scientific research into the spinning golf ball done in the 1890s by Professor Peter Guthrie Tait at Edinburgh University set the sport on a new century of innovation in golf club and ball manufacturing. The learned professor probably has done more than any other single person, before or since, to advance our knowledge of the golf shot.
- The evolution of shot-making in the late 19th century and the 20th century owes much to the professor and his writings.

Chapter 9: Mr. Hogan's Secret Revealed
- After many years of diligent practice that had its share of disappointments, the great Ben Hogan pioneered what we refer to today as the modern swing and stroke.
- Numerous books have been written about the secret of his extraordinary achievements with the golf club. Mr. Hogan himself looked on in amusement as many of the notables in the golfing world beat a path to his door, hoping for some divine inspiration.
- Researching his books and press articles and tracing the evolution of his golf swing, we have been able to identify the secret that the great man never revealed to the media. It was only made possible with the benefit of The Shot-Maker's Code Blueprint.

- Through a lengthy process of experimentation, trial, and error, Mr. Hogan, perhaps unknowingly, emulated the push shot pioneered by the Englishman Harry Vardon over 50 years earlier. Armed with an extended baseline stroke overlaid on the target line, he required only one swing for all his shots. With a small adjustment to the club position and stance alignment during the setup, he was able to fashion any shape or trajectory of shot without any manipulation of the clubface.
- The fundamental swing pioneered by both Messrs Vardon and Hogan is an integral part of The Shot-Maker's Code Blueprint; we call it the baseline precision golf stroke.
- With the extended baseline stroke he used for every shot, Mr. Hogan's dynamic balance was exemplary, as was the precision of his strike.

Chapter 10: Learning Smarter
- The golf shot is mastered by learning the stroke for the shot, not the swing. The motion of the swing automatically responds to the intended stroke.
- The foundation for learning the golf shot is the baseline precision golf stroke. It must be continuously reinforced with practice.
- The shot shape and trajectory are determined not by how the player swings the club or manipulates the clubface but by how he aims, holds, and positions the club during the setup.
- By learning the baseline precision golf stroke and the stroke variable adjustments for shot-making and configuring the setup accordingly, the player has a full armory of shots at his disposal.
- A key element of learning the golf shot is calibrating the baseline precision golf stroke with the target line. An intermediate target is positioned on the ground a foot or so ahead of the ball to assist in the calibration process.

- The diligent and repeated practice and use of the baseline stroke is the key to eliminating the many faults associated with driving from the tee.
- Practice always requires a purpose.
- There are no quick fixes or Band-Aids that can be applied to correct a stroke error or a perceived swing error. The player must recalibrate the baseline stroke to highlight any shortcomings in the setup or takeaway.
- The player must learn to feel the club and stroke and see the shot in his mind's eye. The feel for the shot, and the shot's distance, improves with regular practice on a course the player knows. This is particularly important for the short game and putting.
- The club and the ball must be the appropriate quality and fit for the student to aid learning and facilitate and enhance his feel for the shot. Learning precision distance control on short shots is impossible with an inferior ball.
- Young children learn best by imitating good ball-strikers. They should learn how the ball is struck and practice the baseline stroke, not the swing.
- Young players must have room to develop their swing style and learn the shot, not the swing.
- Skills and experience are gained on the golf course. The golfer must play to learn.

FINAL REMARKS

Writing this book has been a great pleasure for me, and I am indebted to all those who have helped me.

I set out on the task with some trepidation, but I felt compelled to get on with it as I had a story to tell. Previously, I had tried to offer snippets of insights into our discoveries to friends and those prepared to listen. However, I knew that, without a proper context, what I was patiently trying to explain, a knowledge that I had acquired over several years, would never be fully understood.

With the true dynamics of the strike and its importance to the golf shot revealed to Todd and me, I wanted to find a way to reverse engineer the shot and take it back, step-by-step, to its start, the initial visualization of the ball flight, before reversing the process. My son James agreed to help. Without his exemplary ball-striking skills, the task would have been impossible.

Our novel theory of the golf shot emphasizing the role of the stroke and strike dynamics rather than swing and club geometry had to be tested and validated in the real world, on the golf range, and on the golf course. At this point, I am more than happy that we have completed that task.

Some of you might justifiably ask: *"Sounds great for a golf pro, but can this work for me?"* The answer is a resounding yes; it most certainly can.

It requires a change in mindset to view the golf shot as something other than the golf swing. Your thoughts should move away from the swing to the stroke.

The shot-making learning process will be much easier if you understand the fundamentals of the golf stroke, particularly the need for a baseline stroke for every shot. A baseline stroke means that the stroke variability is much less, and the shot is easier to control.

When your attention is on the stroke and your takeaway and follow-through, you will be pleasantly surprised that the swing is intuitive. It will respond naturally to your desired ball flight.

Ben Hogan's secret, the extended baseline stroke, helps to compress the ball fully on the clubface. It is the key to controlling the shot's trajectory and distance in the air and on the ground. Providing the lie is good; there is no reason why the extended baseline stroke shouldn't be incorporated for all full shots, regardless of the standard of the player, the club selected, or the intended shot shape or direction.

Great male and female ball-strikers and shot-makers generally have at least three things in common. Firstly, they all display exquisite balance, rhythm, and tempo; secondly, they all possess an extended takeaway and follow-through; thirdly, they all use the club as a multi-functional precision tool with great feel, imagination, and skill.

With the club operating as a multi-functional tool, exploring the changing and dynamic relationship between the clubhead and clubshaft and its effect on the ball flight will reap dividends for the golfer at any skill level. It requires only a willingness to experiment and learn and let the club work for you.

One final point, to derive maximum benefit, The Shot-Maker's Code has to be used regularly.

If you play a full competitive round at least once a week, you should expect to experience a significant improvement in your scoring in just a few weeks or months. Don't be discouraged if the improvement process takes a little time; with diligent practice and application a whole new golf game awaits you.

I hope you, the reader, will derive much pleasure from your journey of shot-making discovery. Above all, enjoy this great game.

ABOUT THE AUTHOR

The author, right, with 1995 PGA Champion and Vardon Trophy Winner Steve Elkington

Residing in Banchory, Scotland, Paul worked for an Oil and Gas Company in various corporate and project engineering health and safety management roles before retiring in 2006 at age 60. His son James is a professional golfer and was a member of the successful 2011 Great Britain and Ireland Walker Cup team, beating an American team that included Jordan Spieth, Patrick Cantlay, Harris English, and Russell Henley.

Since his retirement, Paul has collaborated extensively with his American colleague, Todd Kos, assisting in his development of analytical tools related to the golf shot.

A former Royal Navy diver, Paul took up sports diving as a hobby after leaving the Navy. He founded and operated Sports Diving Schools in Saudi Arabia and the U.K. and has enjoyed diving in many parts of the world. Paul took up golf after marrying Sue in 1985. Taking an immediate liking to the sport, he introduced his two-year-old son James to the game in 1991.

GLOSSARY OF TERMS

Acceleration	A positive increasing change in the velocity of an object; in golf, usually referring to the hands, arms, or clubhead. Ref. The PGA Manual of Golf 1991.
Angle of Approach, Attack Angle	The angle formed by the descending or ascending arc of the clubhead on the forward swing in relation to the slope of the ground. Ref. The PGA Manual of Golf 1991. Attack Angle is a commonly used metric with launch monitors to describe the angle of approach at the point of impact.
Angular Velocity	A measure of how fast a body rotates about an axis, e.g., revolutions per minute.
Balance Point	The point at which the body is evenly balanced. At address, the player's static balance point is located in the pelvic girdle a few inches below the navel.
Baseline Precision Golf Stroke, Baseline Stroke	The foundation and framework for all full shots, regardless of their intended shape or trajectory. It is configured in advance to deliver the clubface square to the target line at the low point of the swing arc. An extended baseline stroke widens the base of the swing arc, keeping the clubhead stable in the strike zone.
Casting	A premature release of cocked wrists on the forward swing that causes the clubhead to arrive at the ball out of sequence, ahead of the arms and hands. Also known as 'hitting from the top' (early release). Ref. The PGA Manual of Golf 1991.

Center of Gravity (COG)	A point, near or within a body, through which its weight can be assumed to act when considering forces on the body and its motion under gravity. Center of Gravity is often used interchangeably with Center of Mass (COM).
Center of Mass (COM)	The point representing the mean position of the matter in a body.
Centeredness of Contact	The exactness with which the clubface contacts the ball relative to the sweet spot. Contact on the clubface could be on the sweet spot, fore (toe), aft (heel), above, or below. Ref. The PGA Manual of Golf 1991.
Centrifugal Force	A force that acts outwards from its center of rotation, e.g., a whirling weight on a string. An outward throwing action.
Centripetal Force	A force that acts inwards towards its center of rotation to keep an object, e.g., a clubhead, moving on its curved path.
Centrifugal(cf) Release	The centrifugal(cf) release relies on the weight of the arms, club, and clubhead, sustaining the swing's rotation and acceleration.
Centripetal(cp) Release	The centripetal(cp) release relies on the inward pull exerted by the player's powerful core muscles sustaining the swing's rotation and acceleration.
Choke Down	To grip lower on the club for greater control. Ref. The PGA Manual of Golf 1991.
Club Path	A metric in use with launch monitors defining the horizontal direction of the clubhead relative to the target at the point of maximum compression of the golf ball at impact. Positive means right of the target line, while negative means left of the target line.

Clubface Angle	The alignment of the leading edge of the clubface relative to the centerline of the clubshaft, i.e., aligned with it, open or closed to it.
Clubhead Lag	Clubhead lag is when the clubhead trails the grip end of the club on the forward swing. It occurs due to the resistance of the clubhead's inertia to the swing's change in speed and direction.
Clubhead Lag Tension	The tension or stress created in the clubshaft induced by clubhead lag. It sustains the horizontal straight line of compression through the ball, keeping the impact interface stationary and stable.
Clubhead Release Direction	The clubhead release direction is downwards and forwards on the downswing, through impact, into the follow-through.
Clubhead Speed	The speed of the clubhead just prior to first contact with the golf ball in mph.
Compact Swing	A compact swing is typical of today's modern athletic swing. Using an extended takeaway, it has more width than depth.
Compression Torque	When the golfer compresses the clubface with a solid centered strike, any stroke-induced change to the loft of the clubface will generate torque in the ball and determine its resultant spin rate and spin axis. Compression torque can be used to enhance the golfer's control of the shape and trajectory of the shot and determine how far the ball rolls when it lands.

Conical Pendulum Release	The clubhead's automatic, powerful centripetal release is facilitated by the angle retained between the straight left arm and the club.
	The conical pendulum release doesn't involve any active release or manipulation by the hands of the club or clubhead.
Crown	The top surface of a deep-faced clubhead.
Cut	The term cut was originally defined in the early golf manuals as 'An underspin given by a club to a ball.'
	It is also used to describe drawing the clubface across the ball from right to left or to signify a left-to-right curve on the shot.
Divot	A small patch of turf removed by a descending clubhead.
	As the ball is propelled forwards and upwards at impact, the clubhead is pushed down and back, causing the leading edge of the clubface to remove a patch of turf when the ground is soft.
D-Plane	A theoretical mathematical construct published by the American physicist Professor Jorgensen in 1993. It describes the conditions of the collision between the clubhead and the golf ball and the ball's flight. The Physics of Golf, American Institute of Physics, New York, 1994, 1999.
	The D-Plane theory has a modern-day use in launch monitors and informs much of modern-day golf instruction.

Double Pendulum Two-Lever Swing Model	The model describes the lever mechanism of the shoulders, arms, and club on the forward swing. As the upper lever (the shoulders and arms) slows down, the lower lever (the wrists, the club, and the clubhead) speeds up.

The two-lever swing model was designed by scientists to closely approximate the motion of the golf swing. |
| Downward Press | Slight downward pressure is applied to the club with the heel of the left hand to flex the wrists and lift the clubhead off the ground an inch or so before starting the takeaway.

The downward press is associated with the modern swing. |
Drag	An aerodynamic force that resists the forward motion of an object. It influences clubhead speed and ball flight. Ref. The PGA Manual of Golf 1991.
Draw, Draw Shot	A draw is a controlled golf shot that curves slightly from right to left and finishes on or close to the target line.
Dynamic Balance	Transferring the focus of weight approximately during the golf swing while retaining body control. Ref. The PGA Manual of Golf 1991.
Dynamic Loft	The vertical angle of the club face at the center point of contact between the club and ball at the time of maximum compression.

Dynamic Loft is the amount of loft on the club face at impact and is measured relative to the horizon. Ref. Trackman. |

Extended Takeaway and Extended Release	The takeaway is extended when the arms and club are moved back together, with the clubhead leading the hands. Consequently, when the clubhead is released on the downswing, the hands and arms lead the clubhead to extend the clubhead release and sustain lag tension in the clubshaft beyond impact into the follow-through.
Eyeline	The level of the eyes, not the direction in which a person is looking.
Face Angle	Face Angle is the direction the club face is pointed (right or left) at impact and is measured relative to the target line. Ref. Trackman.
Face to Path	The angle between the face angle and the club path at impact.
Fade, Fade Shot	A fade is a controlled golf shot that curves slightly from left to right and finishes on or close to the target line.
Follow-Through	The completion of the stroke, a foot or so after the ball has been struck. The essential movement of the follow-through is the flattening out of the arc described by the clubhead.
Forward Press	A movement, usually with the hands and arms or some other part of the body, assists the player in starting the club away from the ball. Ref. The PGA Manual of Golf, 1991.

The forward press is associated with the traditional rotary swing. It is not relevant to the modern swing and stroke. When combined with a one-piece takeaway, it serves to incorporate a short lateral movement of the clubhead straight back from the ball for a short distance. |

Golf Shot, Shot	Golf shot or shot is often used as a generic term to describe the swing, the strike, and the resultant ball flight.
	It also has specific meanings to describe the outcome of the shot, e.g., shot shape, shot trajectory, shot direction, or the shot type, e.g., cut shot.
Grip Pressure	The firmness or tightness of the grip on the golf club. In the modern swing and stroke, the grip is light, with no trace of undue tension in the wrists and forearms.
Grip Strength	The strength of the grip is gauged by where the V formed between the forefinger and thumb of either hand is pointing when viewed from face on at address. When the V formed between the forefinger and thumb points over the left shoulder, the grip is said to be weak. It is said to be strong when it points over the right shoulder. The grip is neutral when the V points towards the left ear.
Heel	The heel is a specific region of the clubface located between the sweet spot and the hosel.
Hook	A hook is a golf shot that typically derives from a stroke fault and has a pronounced right-to-left curve. A pull hook is a shot that starts to the left of the target and curves even further left.
Hosel	The hosel is the socket in the head of a golf club into which the shaft is inserted.
Impact	The period of time the clubhead remains in contact with the ball when it transfers its energy to the ball.

Kinetic Chain	In the golf swing, the kinetic chain is the different parts of the body acting as a system of chain links to transfer energy through the body from the ground up to the golf club. Energy moves up the chain from one body segment to the next, each movement building upon the previous segment's motion and energy. The entire process is seamless, as the body transfers energy to the clubhead and ball.
Kinetic Energy	The energy an object, e.g., a clubhead, possesses due to its motion.
Laid-Back Cut Stroke, Shot	The laid-back cut stroke or shot uses clubface lay-back at impact to maximize friction force and launch the ball lower at a high speed with maximum backspin. Due to the short flight time, some spin is conserved in the ball and is expressed when the ball lands to stop it quickly or spin it back or to the side. It is a straight shot usually associated with a short approach shot made with a lob wedge from 80 yards or less to the green.
Launch Angle	The ball's initial vertical launch direction relative to the ground level.
Launch Direction	The ball's initial horizontal launch direction relative to the target line.
Launch Monitor	A launch monitor is a device that uses doppler radar, infrared, or high-speed, high-resolution camera technology to precisely measure various aspects of what happens to a golf ball when it is struck by a golf club. It can be used to improve a golfer's swing as part of a lesson or to aid the custom fitting process when purchasing new clubs.
Lie (of the Ball)	The position of the ball after it has come to rest. Ref. The PGA Manual of Golf 1991.

Lie (of the Club)	The angle the clubshaft makes with the clubhead as measured from the center of the clubshaft to a line extending tangentially from the lowest point of the sole. Ref. The PGA Manual of Golf 1991.
Loft	The degree of pitch angle is built into the clubface. Also, to lift a ball into the air with a club. Ref. The PGA Manual of Golf 1991.
Low Point	The low point of the swing arc is reached when the clubhead ends its descent and starts its ascent. It may be on the ground's surface or above it when the ball is teed up. It may be slightly below the ball's surface when a divot is created.
Modern Swing	The modern swing pioneered and popularised by Ben Hogan is a more compact swing and has more width and less depth than the swing types that preceded it. An extended takeaway and an extended follow-through characterize the modern swing. The modern swing is fully automated to precisely deliver the strike to the ball.
Moment of Inertia	A measure of the rotational inertia of a body. A resistance to its change in angular velocity or direction. The longer the moment arm or pivot arm, the greater the resistance.
Momentum, Angular Momentum	In angular motion, momentum is the product of the mass of a body and its angular velocity. A clubhead orbiting around the body has momentum. The rate of change of angular momentum is proportional to the torque acting on the body.
Normal to the Clubface	The angle perpendicular to the flat surface of the clubface.

Off-Center Hit, Mishit	A ball that is not struck with the sweet spot of the clubface. The strike can be higher or lower or on the heel or the toe of the clubface.
One-Piece Takeaway	An early portion of the backswing in which the arms, hands, and wrists move away from the ball in nearly the same relation to each other as they were at address. The wrists may cock very slightly, but neither fan nor hood the face. Ref. The PGA Manual of Golf, 1991.
	The one-piece takeaway is associated with the traditional rotary swing; it is not relevant to the modern swing and stroke.
Power Stroke, Power Shot	A power stroke or power shot releases the clubhead more forwards than downwards, relative to the slope of the ground, through impact. It is facilitated by sighting the back of the ball on its equator, the point on the ball farthest from the target.
	Its purpose is to dynamically change the ball's launch angle and to control how it behaves when it lands, i.e., stopping quickly or rolling more. There are two variants of the shot, the power spinner, and the power runner.
	The power stroke is normally associated with a straight shot with any club. However, as long as the baseline stroke is deployed, it can be used with a draw or a fade.
Push, Push Shot	A push is a straight shot directed to the right of the target line.
	The push shot, not to be confused with the modern term push, was a type of shot in common use at the turn of the 20th Century. Its modern-day equivalent is the power shot.

Rhythm	The synchronization of body and club movements allowing them to rotate in unison at the same rate.
Roll	In a golf context, roll has several meanings.
The rolling of the wrists and forearms. The motion of the ball on the ground after it lands. It also refers to the curvature of the clubface from crown to sole on a driver or other deep-faced club.
Setup	The process followed by the player to hold and position the club and present the clubface to the ball and target. The player's posture, stance, weight distribution, and muscular readiness to execute the shot.
Sightline and Focal Point	The sightline is a hypothetical line perpendicular to the player's eyeline. The sightline directs and projects the focal point, i.e., to the precise point on the ball or close to it. The sightline and focal point are normally established during the setup. They can be adjusted immediately before the start of the downswing.
Slice	A slice is a golf shot that typically derives from a stroke fault and has a pronounced left-to-right curve. A push slice is a shot that starts to the right of the target and curves even further right.
Sole	The sole is the bottom part of the clubhead.
Spin Axis, Spin Axis Tilt	When struck by the clubface, the ball spins about its horizontal axis. The spin axis is tilted to the left or the right to curve the shot.
The amount of spin axis tilt is measured in degrees. A negative sign indicates a tilt to the left, and a positive sign indicates a tilt to the right.

Spin Direction	The ball is struck and compressed on the lofted clubface to generate a backspin. A forward spin will not be created unless the ball is accidentally topped. Because of the loft on the clubface, the ball is normally struck below its equator.
Spin Loft	Spin loft is approximately the angle between the dynamic loft and attack angle
	Spin loft is actually the three-dimensional angle between the direction the club head is moving (both club path and attack angle) and the direction the club face is pointing (both face angle and dynamic loft). Ref. Trackman.
Spin Rate	The ball's rotation speed around its Center of Mass as it leaves the clubface measured in rpm.
Stance	The position of the feet when the player addresses the ball. Ref. The PGA Manual of Golf 1991.
Strike	The term strike may be used in different contexts. As a noun, it refers to the collision between the clubhead and ball with an impact duration lasting for half a millisecond or slightly less. As a verb, it refers to the action of striking the ball, e.g., on a short shot where the hands and wrist muscles are activated to firm up or direct the strike.
Strike Zone	The bottom part of the swing arc. It extends a foot or so on either side of the low point of the swing arc.

Stroke, Golf Stroke	In the modern-day, the stroke is more commonly referred to as the forward motion of the swing. More specifically, it is analogous to the release of the clubhead, initiated during the downswing and completed shortly after impact when the arms and club are fully extended into the follow-through.

Golf's governing bodies define a stroke as 'The forward movement of your club made to strike the ball.' |
| Sweet Spot | The point on the clubface where the clubhead does not torque when struck with a sharp object. The percussion point.

The sweet spot can be projected higher or lower on the clubface depending upon the vertical orientation of the clubhead at impact. |
| Swing Arc | The entire path the clubhead follows on its complete motion away from and towards the target. It has dimensions of both length and width. Ref. The PGA Manual of Golf 1991. |
| Swing Center | The center of rotation of the golf swing located in the rib cage behind the sternal notch.

It is free to move to keep the clubhead on its curved path around the body. |
Swing, Golf Swing	The whole path of the club required to deliver the stroke.
Swing Plane	An imaginary flat, tilted surface used to describe the arc on which the club is swung. The swing is planar only in the bottom half of the swing. It corresponds closely to the clubshaft plane.
Takeaway	The early portion of the backswing. Ref. The PGA Manual of Golf 1991.

Target Line	An imaginary line on the ground connecting the ball to the intended target, where the player wishes the ball to finish its flight.
	The target line is extended behind the ball to facilitate the takeaway.
Tempo	The rotation rate of the swing, e.g., fast or slow.
	An even Tempo to end the backswing and start the forward swing is required to maintain the swing in dynamic balance.
Toe	The toe is a specific region of the clubface located between the sweet spot and the very end of the club. It is the region of the clubface that is located furthest from the golfer.
Torque	The rotational force that causes an object to acquire angular acceleration.
Thoracic Spine	The part of the spine that connects to the rib cage.
Trackman	The first radar launch monitor for golf created in 2003 by brothers Klaus and Morten Eldrup-Jorgensen and radar engineer Fredrik Tuxen.
Trajectory	The path a ball takes in the air. In golf, it relates primarily to the height of the shot. Ref. The PGA Manual of Golf 1991.
Waggle	The rehearsal of the forward motion of the stroke and strike immediately before the start of the extended takeaway.
	To enable the player to feel the heft of the arms and club, the clubhead is raised a foot or so above the ball and lowered before being presented to the ball and target.

REFERENCES

1. Tait, Peter Guthrie. Long Driving, Badminton Magazine, 1896.
2. J.L. Low. F.G. Tait A Record, London 1900.
3. Vardon, Harry. The Complete Golfer, London, 1905.
4. Vardon, Harry. How to Play Golf, Philadelphia, 1912.
5. Vardon, Harry. The Gist of Golf, New York, 1922.
6. Hogan, Ben. Power Golf, New York, 1948, 2010.
7. Hogan, Ben. The Modern Fundamentals of Golf, London, 1957.
8. Jones, Bobby. Golf Is My Game, Chatto & Windus, London, 1959, 1960, 1961.
9. Cochran, A; Stobbs, J. Search for the Perfect Swing, Triumph Books, Chicago, 1968, 2005.
10. Kelley, Homer. The Golfing Machine, The Golfing Machine LLC, Beaverton, Oregon, 1969, 2006.
11. Wiren, Gary. The PGA Manual of Golf, McMillan Publishing Company, New York, 1991.
12. Jorgensen, T. P. The Physics of Golf, American Institute of Physics, New York, 1994, 1999.
13. Elkington, Steve. Five Fundamentals, New York, 1999.
14. Mehlhorn, Bill; Shave, Bobby. Golf Secrets Exposed, M&S Publishing, Miami, Florida, 2001.
15. Tschetter, Kris. Mr. Hogan, The Man I Knew, New York, 2010.

OTHER RESOURCES

1. Farnie, H.B. The Golfer s Manual, London, 1857.
2. McBain, J; Firnie. W. Dean's Championship Handbook of Golf, Edinburgh, 1897.
3. Taylor, J.H. Taylor on Golf. London, 1905.
4. Cargill, Gilston Knott. The Life and Scientific Work of Peter Guthrie Tait. Cambridge University Press, 1911.
5. Vaile, P.A. The Rhythm in Golf, Golf Magazine. New York, August 1916.
6. American Technique, Golf Magazine. New York, August 1916.
7. Morrison, Alex J. A New Way to Better Golf, London, 1932.
8. Jones, Ernest. Swing the Clubhead Method, Nevada, 1937.
9. Cotton, Henry. This Game of Golf, London, 1948.
10. Jacobs, John. Practical Golf, Stanley Paul & Co Ltd, London, 1972.
11. Penick, Harvey; Shrake, Bud. Harvey Penick s Little Red Book, Simon & Schuster, New York, 1992, 2012.
12. Hebron, Michael. Golf Swing Secrets ...And Lies. Six Timeless Lessons, New York, 2001.
13. Vasquez, Jody. Afternoons with Mr. Hogan, Gotham Books, New York, 2004.
14. Burke, Jackie, Jr. It s Only a Game, New York, 2006.
15. Clampett, Bobby; Brumer, Andy. The Impact Zone, New York, 2007.
16. Gould, Steve; Wilkinson, D.J. The Golf Delusion, Elliot & Thompson Ltd, London, 2009.
17. 10 Rules For Hitting All The Shots, Lee Trevino, Golf Digest, 2009.
18. Tischler, Edward A. Secrets of Owning Your Swing, Bloomington, Indiana, 2010.
19. McGee, Seamus. Henry Picard: The Hershey Hurricane, Galde Press, Lakeville, Minnesota, 2011.

20. Maltby, Ralph. Golf Club Fitting and Performance, Newark, Ohio, 2011.
21. Thain, Eric. Science and Golf IV. Proceedings of the World Scientific Congress of Golf, London and New York, 2011.
22. Wright, Mickey. Play Golf the Wright Way, 2013.
23. Hogan's Secret? A Hands-on Approach to Clubfitting, E. Michael Johnson, Golf Digest, 2014.
24. A Brief History of the Golf Ball, Irena Kavas, London, 2016.
25. Trackman Launch Monitor.
26. OptimalFlight and OptimalStrike Golf Shot Analysis Tools.
27. The swingengineer.com. The online home of The Golfing Machine.
28. The Ben Hogan Facebook Page.
29. Jeff Martin's Facebook Page.

YOUTUBE CHANNELS

30. The Golf Shot-Maker's Code
31. Secret Golf
32. Malaska Golf
33. Luther Blacklock Golf
34. Eagolfpro
35. My Swing Evolution
36. Northbound Golf

APPENDIX: CHAPTERS 4 AND 5 SHOT DATA

Data Sources: James Byrne's shot launch data courtesy of an indoor Foresight Sports GCQuad Launch Monitor. Ball flight profiles and downrange results courtesy of the OptimalFlight Analysis Tool.

The shot data presented is an average of ten shots per shot type. A premium golf ball was used, turf hardness was set to standard, no wind.

CHAPTER 4 SHOT LAUNCH DATA, FLIGHT PROFILES, AND DOWNRANGE RESULTS

1. DRAW SHOTS: 6-IRON

The shot data is compared below for a high, medium, and low trajectory draw:

Shot A – 6-Iron High Trajectory Draw Shot
Shot B – 6-Iron Medium Trajectory Draw Shot
Shot C – 6-Iron Low Trajectory Draw Shot

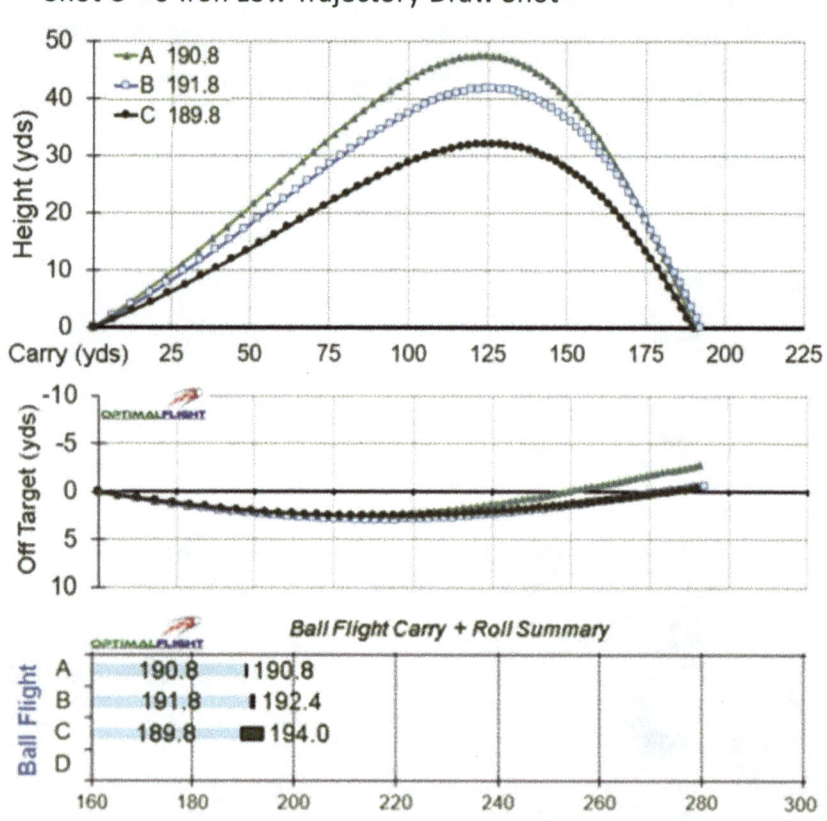

Clubhead Speed and Shot Launch Data	Shot A High Trajectory Draw	Shot B Medium Trajectory Draw	Shot C Low Trajectory Draw
Clubhead Speed (mph)	99.6	99.0	96.1
Ball Speed (mph)	135.1	134.5	132.1
Launch Angle (Degrees)	20.0	17.7	13.0
Launch Direction (Degrees)	+3.6	+3.6	+3.0
Spin Rate (rpm)	5761	5750	5656
Spin Axis Tilt (degrees)	-7.3	-6.3	-5.5

Stable Low Spin Rate for a 6-Iron

Downrange Results	Shot A High Trajectory Draw	Shot B Medium Trajectory Draw	Shot C Low Trajectory Draw
Apex Height (Yards)	47.3	42.7	32.1
Apex Width (Yards)	3.8	3.2	2.6
Landing Angle (Degrees)	50.9	49.5	44.4
Flight Time (Seconds)	7.26	7.02	6.39
Curve Angle (Degrees)	-4.4	-3.8	-3.1
Carry Distance (Yards)	190.8	191.8	189.8
Total Distance (Yards)	190.8	192.4	194.0
Roll Distance (Yards)	0.1	0.6	4.2
Off-Target Carry Distance (Yards)	-2.8	-0.6	-0.4
Off-Target Total Distance (Yards)	-2.8	-0.6	-0.6

Little Difference in Total Distance (3 yards Range)

2. FADE SHOTS: 6-IRON

The shot data is compared below for a high, medium, and low trajectory fade.

Shot A – 6-Iron High Trajectory Fade Shot
Shot B – 6-Iron Medium Trajectory Fade Shot
Shot C – 6-Iron Low Trajectory Fade Shot

Ball Flight Carry + Roll Summary

Ball Flight	Carry	Total
A	176.5	176.5
B	180.5	180.8
C	183.0	185.0

Clubhead Speed and Shot Launch Data	Shot A High Trajectory Fade	Shot B Medium Trajectory Fade	Shot C Low Trajectory Fade
Clubhead Speed (mph)	98.8	98.2	96.6
Ball Speed (mph)	129.1	130.2	130.2
Launch Angle (Degrees)	19.5	17.3	14.0
Launch Direction (Degrees)	-3.5	-2.3	-1.5
Spin Rate (rpm)	6801	6594	6269
Spin Axis Tilt (degrees)	+6.5	+4.0	+3.6

Variable High Spin Rate for a 6-Iron

Downrange Results	Shot A High Trajectory Fade	Shot B Medium Trajectory Fade	Shot C Low Trajectory Fade
Apex Height (Yards)	42.5	39.5	33.4
Apex Width (Yards)	3.0	1.9	1.7
Landing Angle (Degrees)	50.3	48.9	46.1
Flight Time (Seconds)	6.87	6.75	6.42
Curve Angle (Degrees)	3.9	2.4	2.1
Carry Distance (Yards)	176.5	180.5	183.0
Total Distance (Yards)	176.5	180.8	185.0
Roll Distance (Yards)	0.0	0.3	2.0
Off-Target Carry Distance (Yards)	+0.3	+1.8	+1.8
Off-Target Total Distance (Yards)	+0.3	+1.9	+1.9

Marked Differences in Total Distance (10 yards Range)

3. STRAIGHT SHOTS: 6-IRON

The shot data is compared below for a straight, low, medium, and high trajectory shot.

Shot A – 6-Iron Low Trajectory Straight Shot
Shot B – 6-Iron Medium Trajectory Straight Shot
Shot C – 6-Iron High Trajectory Straight Shot

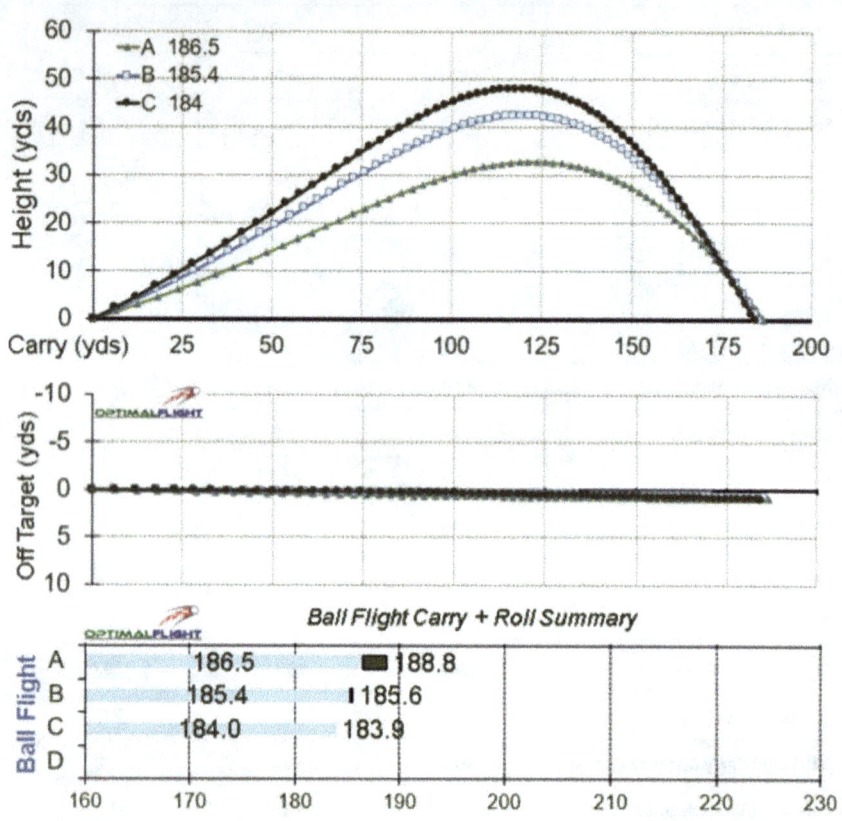

Clubhead Speed and Shot Launch Data	Shot A Low Trajectory Straight Shot	Shot B Medium Trajectory Straight Shot	Shot C High Trajectory Straight Shot
Clubhead Speed (mph)	97.3	99.0	100.2
Ball Speed (mph)	132.0	132.7	133.3
Launch Angle (Degrees)	13.1	18.0	20.9
Launch Direction (Degrees)	+0.5	+0.2	0.0
Spin Rate (rpm)	6178	6290	6228
Spin Axis Tilt (Degrees)	-0.4	0.0	+0.5

Stable Average Spin Rate for 6-Iron

Downrange Results	Shot A Low Trajectory Straight Shot	Shot B Medium Trajectory Straight Shot	Shot C High Trajectory Straight Shot
Apex Height (Yards)	32.9	42.5	48.2
Apex Width (Yards)	0.2	0.0	0.2
Landing Angle (Degrees)	45.6	49.6	51.3
Time of Flight (Seconds)	6.42	6.96	7.26
Curve Angle (Degrees)	-0.2	0.0	+0.3
Carry Distance (Yards)	186.5	185.4	184.0
Total Distance (Yards)	188.8	185.6	183.9
Roll Distance (Yards)	2.3	0.2	-0.1
Off-Target Carry Distance (Yards)	+0.9	+0.6	+0.9
Off-Target Total Distance (Yards)	+0.9	+0.6	+0.9

Marginal Differences in Total Distance (5 yards Range)

SHOT DATA ANALYSES AND KEY OBSERVATIONS

The variability in spin rate and carry distance of the differing shot types executed with the same club makes distance control challenging, especially when other factors, such as the wind, must be considered. The player would be advised to choose a favored stock shot to help assure the reliability and consistency of the shot and change the shot only when necessary, e.g., negotiating a hazard.

Alternatively, the player may wish to have the full portfolio of shots available to him. He then has the option of choosing a low shot or a draw to increase the shot's distance when 'between clubs', or a high shot or fade to reduce it.

Golf science today is evolving at an incredible pace with all kinds of data presented. Generating data is not a problem. Understanding it is a challenge. Golf secrets often do not have data to back them up. We are constantly struggling with an incomplete story to explain what works and what doesn't.

Motion capture and force measuring systems, and robotic devices, no matter how advanced and lifelike, will not teach you what you can learn from The Shot-Maker's Code. It would take a great amount of coordination and expense to model and simulate the simple things that golfers do naturally, such as tilt the clubshaft, adjust the grip position, and execute a balanced swing.

Here is a summary of launch data and downrange results for each of the nine shots contained in The Shot-Maker's Matrix from Chapter 3, shown here for reference.

The Shot-Maker's Matrix
(Right-Handed Player)

Clubshaft Tilt Adjustment (Clubface Aligned to Target) \ Right-Hand Grip Strength Adjustment	Weak	Neutral	Strong
Forward	Low Trajectory Straight Shot	Low Trajectory Draw Shot	Medium Trajectory Draw Shot
Neutral	Low Trajectory Fade Shot	Medium Trajectory Straight Shot	High Trajectory Draw Shot
Rearward	Medium Trajectory Fade Shot	High Trajectory Fade Shot	High Trajectory Straight Shot

Note: The baseline precision golf stroke is the foundation for the variable stroke adjustments for shot-making.

☐ Straight Shot
☐ Fade Shot
☐ Draw Shot

Launch Angle

Note how the medium trajectory shots are similar in launch angle at approximately 17.3-18.0 degrees.

6I Shot Matrix – Launch Angle (degrees)				6I Shot Matrix – Launch Angle (degrees)		
13.1 Weak + Forward	13.0 Neutral + Forward	17.7 Strong + Forward		19.5 High Fade	20.9 High Straight	20 High Draw
14.0 Weak + Neutral	18.0 Neutral + Neutral	20.0 Strong + Neutral		17.3 Med Fade	18.0 Med Straight	17.7 Med Draw
17.3 Weak + Rearward	19.5 Neutral + Rearward	20.9 Strong + Rearward		14.0 Low Fade	13.1 Low Straight	13.0 Low Draw

Left table: Clubshaft Tilt (Rearward, Neutral, Forward) × Right Hand Grip Strength (Weak, Neutral, Strong)

Right table: Shot Trajectory (Low, Med, High) × Shot Type (Fade, Straight, Draw)

Launch Direction

The draws started the ball to the right, while the fades started to the left. Straight shots at varying trajectories went straight.

6I Shot Matrix – Launch Direction (degrees)				6I Shot Matrix – Launch Direction (degrees)		
0.5 Weak + Forward	3.0 Neutral + Forward	3.6 Strong + Forward		-3.5 High Fade	0.0 High Straight	3.6 High Draw
-1.5 Weak + Neutral	0.2 Neutral + Neutral	3.6 Strong + Neutral		-2.3 Med Fade	0.2 Med Straight	3.6 Med Draw
-2.3 Weak + Rearward	-3.5 Neutral + Rearward	0.0 Strong + Rearward		-1.5 Low Fade	0.5 Low Straight	3.0 Low Draw

Left table: Clubshaft Tilt (Rearward, Neutral, Forward) × Right Hand Grip Strength (Weak, Neutral, Strong)

Right table: Shot Trajectory (Low, Med, High) × Shot Type (Fade, Straight, Draw)

Curve Angle

The Curve Angle is a novel metric provided by the OptimalFlight Analysis Tool. It explains how much the ball flight curves away from its start line (Launch Direction). If the Curve Angle + Launch Direction = zero, the shot lands on or very near the target.

The Curve Angle simplifies the ball flight information and makes it easier to understand. The spin rate and spin axis data alone don't provide this information.

Clubshaft Tilt (Rearward, Neutral, Forward)	6I Shot Matrix – Curve Angle (degrees)		
	-0.2 Weak + Forward	-3.1 Neutral + Forward	-3.8 Strong + Forward
	2.1 Weak + Neutral	0.0 Neutral + Neutral	-4.4 Strong + Neutral
	2.4 Weak + Rearward	3.9 Neutral + Rearward	0.3 Strong + Rearward
	Right Hand Grip Strength (Weak, Neutral, Strong)		

Shot Trajectory (Low, Med, High)	6I Shot Matrix – Curve Angle (degrees)		
	3.9 High Fade	0.3 High Straight	-4.4 High Draw
	2.4 Med Fade	0.0 Med Straight	-3.8 Med Draw
	2.1 Low Fade	-0.2 Low Straight	-3.1 Low Draw
	Shot Type (Fade, Straight, Draw)		

On-Target Result - Curve Angle (CA) + Launch Direction (LD)

This measure is useful so you can understand how on-target your results are. If you send the ball right at 3°, and it curves back -3°, it lands on target.

All the average results are within one degree of the downrange target. Show me a robot that can achieve this accuracy with nine distinctly different flight paths.

6I Shot Matrix – Curve Angle + Launch Direction (degrees)				6I Shot Matrix – Curve Angle + Launch Direction (degrees)		
0.3 Weak + Forward	-0.1 Neutral + Forward	-0.2 Strong + Forward		0.4 High Fade	0.3 High Straight	-0.8 High Draw
0.6 Weak + Neutral	0.2 Neutral + Neutral	-0.8 Strong + Neutral		0.1 Med Fade	0.2 Med Straight	-0.2 Med Draw
0.1 Weak + Rearward	0.4 Neutral + Rearward	0.3 Strong + Rearward		0.6 Low Fade	0.3 Low Straight	-0.1 Low Draw
Right Hand Grip Strength (Weak, Neutral, Strong)				Shot Type (Fade, Straight, Draw)		

Left table row labels (Clubshaft Tilt: Rearward, Neutral, Forward). Right table row labels (Shot Trajectory: Low, Med, High).

Ball Speed

Consistent results at different straight-shot trajectories were achieved. The highest ball speeds were with neutral and forward clubshaft tilt and a strong right-hand grip position.

6I Shot Matrix – Ball Speed (rpm)				6I Shot Matrix – Ball Speed (rpm)		
132.0 Weak + Forward	132.1 Neutral + Forward	134.5 Strong + Forward		129.1 High Fade	133.3 High Straight	135.1 High Draw
130.2 Weak + Neutral	132.7 Neutral + Neutral	135.1 Strong + Neutral		130.2 Med Fade	132.7 Med Straight	134.5 Med Draw
130.2 Weak + Rearward	129.1 Neutral + Rearward	133.33 Strong + Rearward		130.2 Low Fade	132.0 Low Straight	132.1 Low Draw
Right Hand Grip Strength (Weak, Neutral, Strong)				Shot Type (Fade, Straight, Draw)		

Carry Distance

Carry results were consistent for straight shots. What is different is that the downrange carry + roll will vary.

6I Shot Matrix – Carry Distance (yards)				6I Shot Matrix – Carry Distance (yards)		
Clubshaft Tilt (Rearward, Neutral, Forward)	186.5 Weak + Forward	189.8 Neutral + Forward	191.8 Strong + Forward	**Shot Trajectory** (Low, Med, High)	176.5 High Fade	184.0 High Straight	190.8 High Draw
	183.0 Weak + Neutral	185.4 Neutral + Neutral	190.8 Strong + Neutral		180.5 Med Fade	185.4 Med Straight	191.8 Med Draw
	180.5 Weak + Rearward	176.5 Neutral + Rearward	184.0 Strong + Rearward		183.0 Low Fade	186.5 Low Straight	189.8 Low Draw
Right Hand Grip Strength (Weak, Neutral, Strong)				Shot Type (Fade, Straight, Draw)		

Total Distance – Carry Distance + Roll

The low shots had more roll than the high trajectory shots, which is expected due to the lower landing angles of the ball. This can be very useful when you want precise control of the ball downrange (stopping on the green or landing and some extra yards). What is impressive is that a range of total distances from 176.6 to 194.0 yards is happening from the same baseline stroke under different stroke variable configurations.

6I Shot Matrix – Total Distance (yards)				6I Shot Matrix – Total Distance (yards)		
Clubshaft Tilt (Rearward, Neutral, Forward)	188.8 Weak + Forward	194.0 Neutral + Forward	192.4 Strong + Forward	**Shot Trajectory** (Low, Med, High)	176.5 High Fade	183.9 High Straight	190.8 High Draw
	185.0 Weak + Neutral	185.6 Neutral + Neutral	190.8 Strong + Neutral		180.8 Med Fade	185.6 Med Straight	192.4 Med Draw
	180.8 Weak + Rearward	176.5 Neutral + Rearward	183.9 Strong + Rearward		185.0 Low Fade	188.8 Low Straight	194.0 Low Draw
Right Hand Grip Strength (Weak, Neutral, Strong)				Shot Type (Fade, Straight, Draw)		

Spin Axis Tilt Angle

The spin axis was tilted for draws and fades. No question about that! What this metric does not tell you is how offline the result is, unlike the curve angle data.

6I Shot Matrix – Tilt Angle (degrees)				6I Shot Matrix – Tilt Angle (degrees)		
-0.4 Weak + Forward	-5.5 Neutral + Forward	-6.3 Strong + Forward		6.5 High Fade	0.5 High Straight	-7.3 High Draw
3.6 Weak + Neutral	0.0 Neutral + Neutral	-7.3 Strong + Neutral		4.0 Med Fade	0.0 Med Straight	-6.3 Med Draw
4.0 Weak + Rearward	6.5 Neutral + Rearward	0.5 Strong + Rearward		3.6 Low Fade	-0.4 Low Straight	-5.5 Low Draw

Left table: Clubshaft Tilt (Rearward, Neutral, Forward) vs. Right Hand Grip Strength (Weak, Neutral, Strong)

Right table: Shot Trajectory (Low, Med, High) vs. Shot Type (Fade, Straight, Draw)

Total Spin Rate

It shows deliberate control of spin for fades, straights, and draws. The most spin was generated from the High Fade shot. As a result, it was the shortest shot result of the nine configurations.

6I Shot Matrix – Total Spin Rate (rpm)				6I Shot Matrix – Total Spin Rate (rpm)		
6178.0 Weak + Forward	5656.0 Neutral + Forward	5750.0 Strong + Forward		6801.0 High Fade	6228.0 High Straight	5761.0 High Draw
6269.0 Weak + Neutral	6290.0 Neutral + Neutral	5761.0 Strong + Neutral		6594.0 Med Fade	6290.0 Med Straight	5750.0 Med Draw
6594.0 Weak + Rearward	6801.0 Neutral + Rearward	6228.0 Strong + Rearward		6269.0 Low Fade	6178.0 Low Straight	5656.0 Low Draw

Left table: Clubshaft Tilt (Rearward, Neutral, Forward) vs. Right Hand Grip Strength (Weak, Neutral, Strong)

Right table: Shot Trajectory (Low, Med, High) vs. Shot Type (Fade, Straight, Draw)

DATA VALIDATION CONCLUSIONS

The shot data has been validated, showing how The Shot-Maker's Code can give a golfer the proper shot-making fundamentals to produce an exciting range of shots, curved or straight, to reach the target.

CHAPTER 5 SHOT LAUNCH DATA, FLIGHT PROFILES, AND DOWNRANGE RESULTS

1. 6-IRON: POWER SPINNER

The power spinner is derived from a setup for a low straight shot.

The shot data compares the power spinner to its derivative, the low straight shot

Shot A – 6-Iron Low Straight Shot
Shot B – 6-Iron Power Spinner

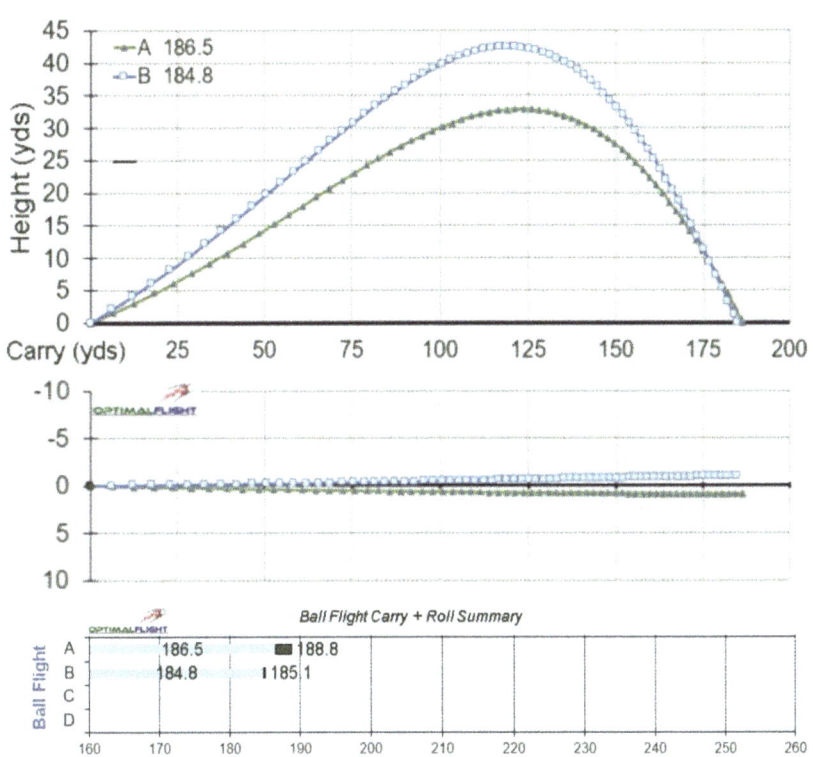

Clubhead Speed and Ball Launch Data	Shot A 6 Iron Low Straight Shot	Shot B 6 Iron Power Spinner
Clubhead Speed (mph)	97.3	98.3
Ball Speed (mph)	132.0	131.7
Launch Angle (Degrees)	13.1	18.4
Launch Direction (Degrees)	+0.5	-0.2
Spin Rate (rpm)	6178	6112
Spin Axis Tilt (degrees)	-0.4	-0.2

Downrange Results	Shot A 6 Iron Low Straight Shot	Shot B 6 Iron Power Spinner
Apex Height (Yards)	32.9	42.5
Apex Width (Yards)	0.2	0.1
Landing Angle (Degrees)	45.6	49.6
Time of Flight (Seconds)	6.42	6.95
Curve Angle (Degrees)	-0.2	-0.1
Carry Distance (Yards)	186.5	184.8
Total Distance (Yards)	188.8	185.1
Roll Distance (Yards)	2.3	0.3
Off-Target Carry Distance (Yards)	+0.9	-1.0
Off-Target Total Distance (Yards)	+0.9	-1.0

Note the stopping power of the Power Spinner

Key Observations

The power spinner is nearly 4 yards shorter overall than the low straight shot but has a much shorter stopping distance, enhancing the player's control of distance.

2. THE DRIVER: POWER RUNNER

The power runner converts a high straight shot into a long, powerful mid-trajectory shot. The launch data, flight profile, and downrange results for a high straight shot are also included for comparison.

Shot A – Driver High Straight Shot
Shot B – Driver Power Runner

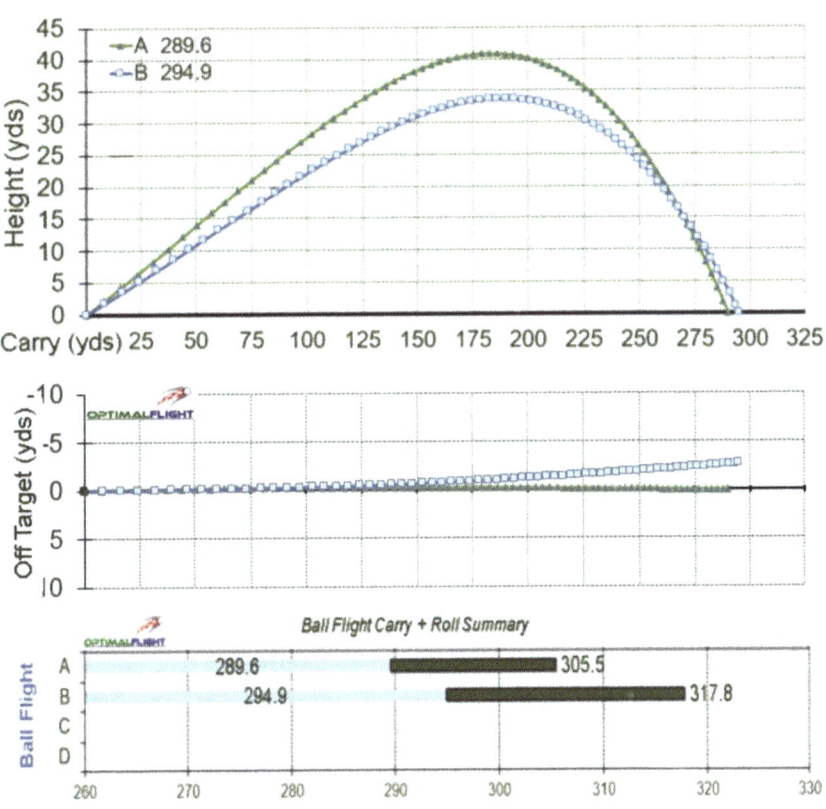

Clubhead Speed and Launch Data	Shot A Driver High Straight Shot	Shot B Driver Power Runner
Clubhead Speed	118.1	119.9
Ball Speed (mph)	166.7	174.4
Launch Angle (Degrees)	15.3	11.9
Launch Direction (Degrees)	-0.2	0
Spin Rate (rpm)	2077	2014
Spin Axis Tilt (Degrees)	+0.5	-1.5
Downrange Results	Shot A Driver High Straight Shot	Shot B Driver Power Runner
Apex Height (Yards)	40.9	33.7
Apex Width (Yards)	0.3	0.7
Landing Angle (Degrees)	39.5	35.1
Flight Time (Seconds)	7.08	6.65
Curve Angle (Degrees)	+0.2	-0.5
Carry Distance (Yards)	289.6	294.9
Total Distance (Yards)	305.5	317.8
Roll Distance (Yards)	15.9	22.9
Off-Target Carry Distance (Yards)	+0.1	-2.7
Off-Target Total Distance (Yards)	+0.2	-3.1

Note the increased carry distance and roll accompanying a lower shot trajectory

Key Observations

The marked difference in ball speed for Shot B, the power runner, stands out with only a marginal difference in clubhead speed, a clear indication that the power runner, when executed correctly, delivers more energy to the ball. It should be noted that because of the higher ball speed and lower launch angle, the lower power runner obtains significantly more carry distance and roll than the high straight shot.

3. DRIVER: SHAPING THE POWER SHOT

A power shot is shaped by pivoting the stance hips and shoulders more open for a fade and less open for a draw. The launch data, flight profile, and downrange results for a power fade and a power draw are shown. The power runner with the driver is included for comparison.

Shot A – Driver Power Fade
Shot B – Driver Power Runner
Shot C – Driver Power Draw

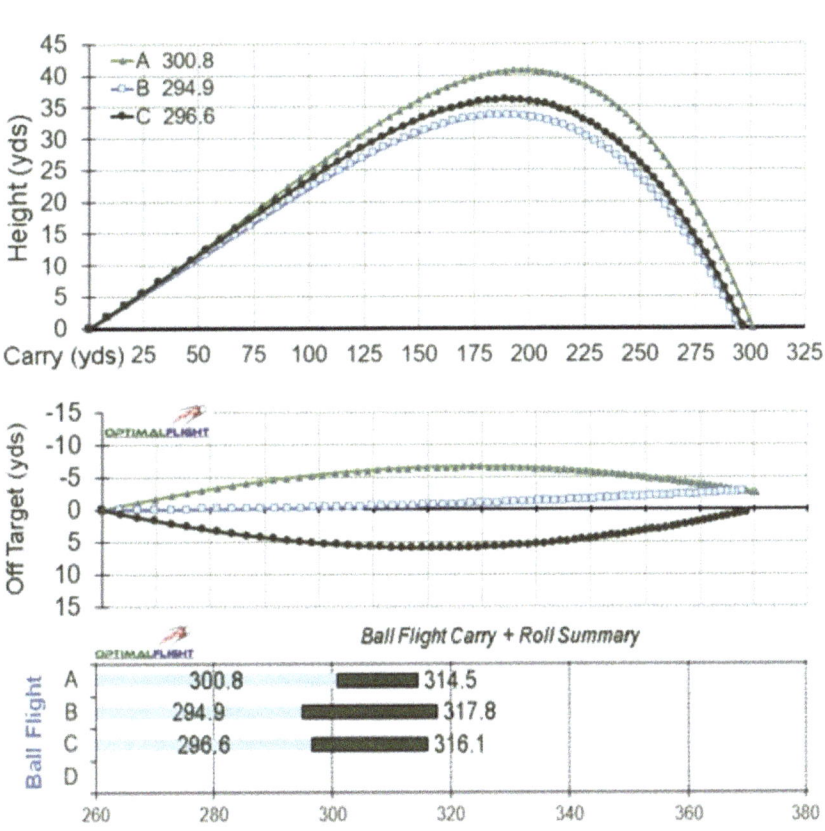

Clubhead Speed and Shot Launch Data	Shot A Driver Power Fade	Shot B Driver Power Runner	Shot C Driver Power Draw
Clubhead Speed (mph)	120.7	119.9	121.2
Ball Speed (mph)	175.3	174.4	174.6
Launch Angle (Degrees)	12.6	11.9	12.7
Launch Direction (Degrees)	-4.2	0	4.3
Spin Rate (rpm)	2584	2014	2090
Spin Axis Tilt (Degrees)	+8.2	-1.5	-10.9
Downrange Results	Shot A Driver Power Fade	Shot B Driver Power Runner	Shot C Driver Power Draw
Apex Height (Yards)	40.8	33.7	36.1
Apex Width (Yards	5.1	0.7	5.7
Landing Angle (Degrees)	40.3	35.1	37.1
Flight Time (Seconds)	7.36	6.65	6.82
Curve Angle (Degrees)	+3.7	-0.5	-4.2
Carry Distance (Yards)	300.8	294.9	296.6
Total Distance (Yards)	314.5	317.8	316.1
Roll Distance (Yards)	13.7	22.9	19.6
Off-Target Carry Distance (Yards)	-2.5	-2.7	+0.4
Off-Target Total Distance (Yards)	-1.8	-3.1	-1.0

Comparable Total Distance

Key Observations

While there is a difference in the height of each shot due to the variation in spin rate, there is only a marginal difference in ball speed and the overall distance. The data strongly suggests that the power stroke be used to shape the shot and reduce the variability in overall distance from the tee.

4. THE SHORT PUNCH SHOT AND THE SHORT RUNNING PITCH SHOT

The punch shot, designed to stop the ball quickly on landing, is compared to the choked-down running pitch shot aimed at landing the ball on the green and rolling it toward the hole.

Shot A – 56° Sand Wedge Short Punch Shot
Shot B – 52° Gap Wedge Short Running Pitch Shot

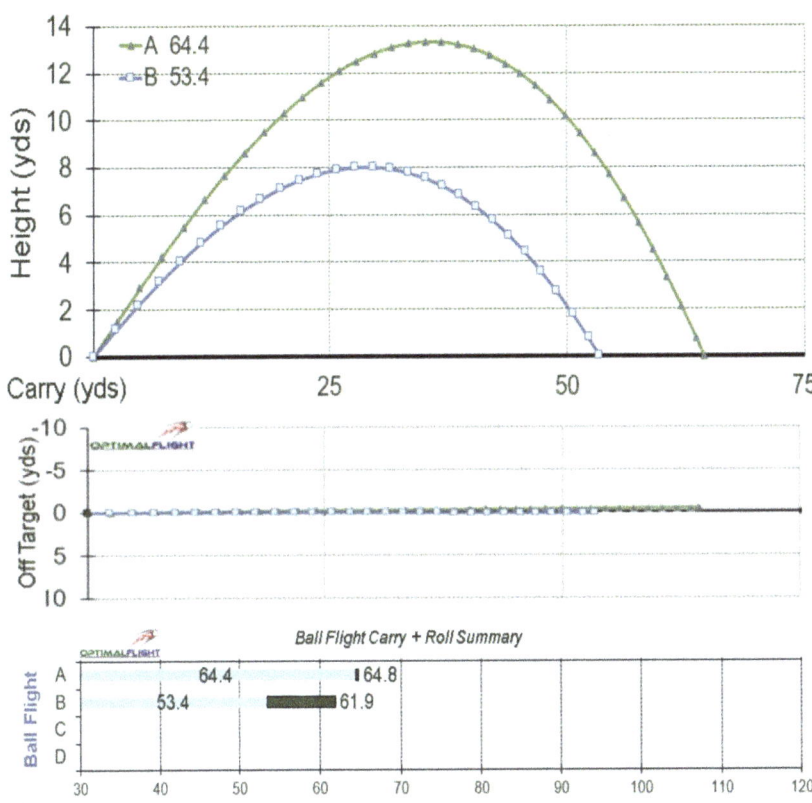

Clubhead Speed and Shot Launch Data	Shot A 56° Sand Wedge Short Punch Shot	Shot B 52° Gap Wedge Short Running Pitch Shot
Clubhead Speed (mph)	61.0	47.3
Ball Speed (mph)	60.1	54.5
Launch Angle (Degrees)	31.9	26.4
Launch Direction (Degrees)	-0.5	0.0
Spin Rate (rpm)	7912	5414
Spin Axis Tilt (Degrees)	+0.5	+1.1
Downrange Results	Shot A 56° Sand Wedge Short Punch Shot	Shot B 52° Gap Wedge Short Running Pitch Shot
Apex Height (Yards)	13.3	8.0
Apex Width (Yards)	0.0	0.0
Landing Angle (Degrees)	42.2	32.5
Flight Time (Seconds)	3.56	2.77
Curve Angle (Degrees)	+0.1	+0.2
Carry Distance (Yards)	64.4	53.4
Total Distance (Yards)	64.8	61.9
Roll Distance (Yards)	0.4	8.5
Off-Target Carry Distance (Yards)	-0.4	+0.2
Off-Target Total Distance (Yards)	-0.4	+0.3

Compare roll distances

Key Observations

The spin rate is the clear difference between the two shots, apart from the shot's height and carry distance. The spin rate for the running pitch shot is more than 2,000 rpm lower than the spin for the short punch shot.

Both shots obtain a similar total distance at just over 60 yards with 3 yards between them. The running pitch rolls 8.5 yards on landing, compared to less than half a yard for the short punch shot.

5. THE SHORT, LAID-BACK CUT SHOT AND LOW SPINNER

The shot data for the short, laid-back cut shot and the low spinner with a 60° lob wedge is compared to a normal full shot with the same club.

Shot A – 60° Wedge Full Shot
Shot B – 60° Wedge Short-Laid Back Cut Shot
Shot C – 60° Wedge Short Low Spinner

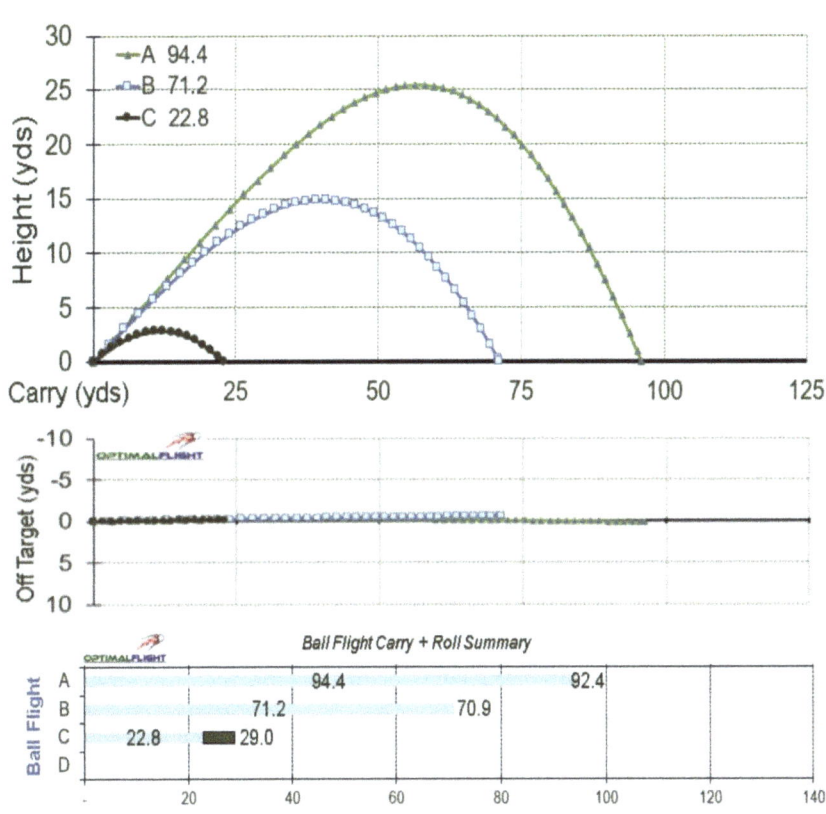

Clubhead Speed and Shot Launch Data	Shot A 60° Wedge 95 Yard Normal Full Shot	Shot B 60° Wedge 70 Yard Short Laid-Back Cut Shot	Shot C 60° Wedge 30 Yard Low Spinner
Clubhead Speed (mph)	88.6	69.7	37.7
Ball Speed (mph)	81.0	64.7	35.5
Launch Angle (Degrees)	31.2	30.6	25.4
Launch Direction (Degrees)	-0.6	-0.8	-0.6
Spin Rate (rpm)	12197	9664	5387
Spin Axis Tilt (Degrees)	+1.7	+1.2	+3.5

The optimal launch angle for a short high-spinning wedge shot is around 30° or less

Downrange Results	Shot A 60° Wedge 95 Yard Normal Full Shot	Shot B 60° Wedge 70 Yard Short Laid-Back Cut Shot	Shot C 60° Wedge 30 Yard Low Spinner
Apex Height (Yards)	24.8	14.8	2.9
Apex Width (Yards)	0.3	0.1	0.0
Landing Angle (Degrees)	50.3	43.8	25.7
Flight Time (Seconds)	4.98	3.81	1.57
Curve Angle (Degrees)	+0.7	+0.3	+0.3
Carry Distance (Yards)	94.4	71.2	22.8
Total Distance (Yards)	92.4	70.9	29.0
Roll Distance (Yards)	-2.0	-0.4	6.2
Off-Target Carry Distance (Yards)	+0.1	-0.6	-0.1
Off-Target Total Distance (Yards)	+0.1	-0.6	-0.1

The ball stops on the 2nd bounce and may spin back

The ball rolls and slows its advance after the 2nd bounce

Key Observations

The longer 70-yard laid-back cut shot has enough spin conserved during its flight to spin the ball back a little on landing. The much shorter 30-yard low spinner has a lower spin rate, but it is enough to slow the ball and stop it fairly quickly after its second bounce. If needed, the ball can be stopped sooner by weakening the grip further and opening the clubface.

Note how the lower spinner has a positive spin axis tilt of +3.5 degrees with only a small curve on the shot, +0.3 degrees curve angle. This is explained by the low ball speed. The speed of airflow passing the ball is not high enough to curve the shot.

The optimal launch angle for a short, laid-back cut shot is around 30 degrees or less.

www.ingramcontent.com/pod-product-compliance
Lightning Source LLC
Chambersburg PA
CBHW071731150426
43191CB00027B/1157